Secrets of the Trade

by Jonathan Tolins

A Samuel French Acting Edition

New York Hollywood London Toronto

SAMUELFRENCH.COM

Copyright © 2011 by Jonathan Tolins
ALL RIGHTS RESERVED

CAUTION: Professionals and amateurs are hereby warned that *SECRETS OF THE TRADE* is subject to a licensing fee. It is fully protected under the copyright laws of the United States of America, the British Commonwealth, including Canada, and all other countries of the Copyright Union. All rights, including professional, amateur, motion picture, recitation, lecturing, public reading, radio broadcasting, television and the rights of translation into foreign languages are strictly reserved. In its present form the play is dedicated to the reading public only.

The amateur and professional live stage performance rights to *SECRETS OF THE TRADE* are controlled exclusively by Samuel French, Inc., and licensing arrangements and performance licenses must be secured well in advance of presentation. PLEASE NOTE that amateur licensing fees are set upon application in accordance with your producing circumstances. When applying for a licensing quotation and a performance license please give us the number of performances intended, dates of production, your seating capacity and admission fee. Licensing fees are payable one week before the opening performance of the play to Samuel French, Inc., at 45 W. 25th Street, New York, NY 10010.

Licensing fee of the required amount must be paid whether the play is presented for charity or gain and whether or not admission is charged.

Professional/Stock licensing fees quoted upon application to Samuel French, Inc.

For all other rights than those stipulated above, apply to: William Morris Endeavor Entertainment, 1325 Avenue of the Americas, New York, NY 10019; attn: Derek Zasky.

Particular emphasis is laid on the question of amateur or professional readings, permission and terms for which must be secured in writing from Samuel French, Inc.

Copying from this book in whole or in part is strictly forbidden by law, and the right of performance is not transferable.

Whenever the play is produced the following notice must appear on all programs, printing and advertising for the play: "Produced by special arrangement with Samuel French, Inc."

Due authorship credit must be given on all programs, printing and advertising for the play.

ISBN 978-0-573-69932-0   Printed in U.S.A.   #29882

> No one shall commit or authorize any act or omission by which the copyright of, or the right to copyright, this play may be impaired.

> No one shall make any changes in this play for the purpose of production.

> Publication of this play does not imply availability for performance. Both amateurs and professionals considering a production are strongly advised in their own interests to apply to Samuel French, Inc., for written permission before starting rehearsals, advertising, or booking a theatre.

> No part of this book may be reproduced, stored in a retrieval system, or transmitted in any form, by any means, now known or yet to be invented, including mechanical, electronic, photocopying, recording, videotaping, or otherwise, without the prior written permission of the publisher.

MUSIC USE NOTE

Licensees are solely responsible for obtaining formal written permission from copyright owners to use copyrighted music in the performance of this play and are strongly cautioned to do so. If no such permission is obtained by the licensee, then the licensee must use only original music that the licensee owns and controls. Licensees are solely responsible and liable for all music clearances and shall indemnify the copyright owners of the play and their licensing agent, Samuel French, Inc., against any costs, expenses, losses and liabilities arising from the use of music by licensees.

IMPORTANT BILLING AND CREDIT REQUIREMENTS

All producers of *SECRETS OF THE TRADE must* give credit to the Author of the Play in all programs distributed in connection with performances of the Play, and in all instances in which the title of the Play appears for the purposes of advertising, publicizing or otherwise exploiting the Play and/or a production. The name of the Author *must* appear on a separate line on which no other name appears, immediately following the title and *must* appear in size of type not less than fifty percent of the size of the title type.

In addition the following credit *must* be given in all programs and publicity information distributed in association with this piece:

New York Premiere produced by Primary Stages
(Casey Childs, Founder and Executive Producer;
Andrew Leynse, Artistic Director; Elliot Fox, Managing Director),
in association with Ted Snowdon Productions, August 2010

Originally produced by the Black Dahlia Theatre, Los Angeles, CA

Originally Commissioned by South Coast Repertory

The world premiere of ***SECRETS OF THE TRADE*** was presented at The Black Dahlia Theatre in California (Matt Shakman, Artistic Director; Jennifer Welsh, Producer) on March 15, 2008. The performance was directed by Matt Shakman, with scenic design by Craig Siebels, lighting by Mike Durst, costume design by E.B. Brooks, original music and sound by Joel Spence, projections by Michele Miatello, and casting by Jeff Greenberg. The production stage managers were Susan Coulter and Breanna Mowdy.

PETER LIPMAN	Mark L. Taylor
ANDREW LIPMAN	Edward Tournier
JOANNE LIPMAN	Amy Aquino
BRADLEY	Bill Brochtrup
MARTIN KERNER	John Glover

SECRETS OF THE TRADE was presented by Primary Stages (Casey Childs, Founder and Executive Producer; Andrew Leynse, Artistic Director; Elliot Fox, Managing Director), in association with Ted Snowdon, at 59E59 Theaters, New York City, on August 10, 2010. The performance was directed by Matt Shakman, with scenic design by Mark Worthington, costume design by Alejo Vietti, lighting by Mike Durst, original music and sound design by John Gromada, and casting by Stephanie Klapper Casting. The production stage manager was Sarah Caddell. The cast was as follows:

PETER LIPMAN	Mark Nelson
ANDREW LIPMAN	Noah Robbins
JOANNE LIPMAN	Amy Aquino
BRADLEY	Bill Brochtrup
MARTIN KERNER	John Glover

CHARACTERS

ANDREW LIPMAN - A precocious boy from Long Island. He begins the play at sixteen.

JOANNE LIPMAN - His mother, a high school teacher and former dancer.

PETER LIPMAN - Andy's father, an architect.

MARTIN KERNER - A famous writer and director for the Broadway stage. A brilliant and charismatic older man.

BRADLEY - Kerner's personal assistant of many years.

SETTING

New York, California, and Massachusetts.

TIME

1980-1990

AUTHOR'S NOTE

This play is, in part, about the magic of the theater. It should, therefore, be staged with only suggestions of scenery that evoke time and place in a creative and theatrical way. The passage of time should be conveyed subtly through costume and style. Andy is the only character who goes through a significant change in his bearing and appearance through the course of the performance.

For my teachers.

ACT ONE

Scene One

(In the dark: We hear music – energetic, both sweet and sour – and a snippet from a classical or public radio news program circa 1980. Something about Reagan.)

(At rise: **ANDREW LIPMAN**, *16, is finishing dinner with his parents,* **JOANNE** *and* **PETER**. *There is clearly a base of love between these three, despite the fact that* **ANDREW** *is at the age at which he is intensely embarrassed by everything his parents say. A copy of* The New York Times *is on the table.)*

PETER. So write him a letter.

ANDY. I don't know…

PETER. Why not?

JOANNE. If he doesn't want to, don't push him.

PETER. Maybe he needs to be pushed. This could be a great opportunity. To work with somebody like Martin Kerner, at this stage in his life…

ANDY. Martin Kerner doesn't want me…

PETER. How do you know? He'd be lucky to get you. He'd learn from you.

ANDY. Dad, stop, all right? I hate it when you do this…

PETER. All right, all right. He's so sensitive.

JOANNE. You want more?

ANDY. What would I write?

PETER. Tell him you're a fan, whatever. That you read in the *Times* he's doing the show in London and you want to work for him.

JOANNE. Just be yourself.

PETER. Tell him that your version at Schreiber High School was better than his on Broadway.

ANDY. It was not! Dad!

JOANNE. Peter, don't tease him.

PETER. I'm not teasing him. I'm entitled to my opinion.

ANDY. Mom! He says these things that make me crazy, it's like…God. Yeah, I'll write, "Dear Mr. Kerner, congratulations on winning six Tony awards for both writing and directing. By the way, my father says you could use my help."

PETER. That's not bad.

ANDY. Will you…? Just…don't!

JOANNE. I liked yours better, too.

PETER. See that?

ANDY. Denise Kaplan couldn't remember her lines.

PETER. Even so. What you did on that stage with no money…

JOANNE. Yours had more heart.

PETER. No question.

JOANNE. But maybe we're biased a little.

ANDY. I'm done. Can I go?

JOANNE. Do your homework.

ANDY. *(dismissive)* Please.

(ANDY rises and exits, taking the newspaper with him.)

JOANNE. Are you sure that's a good idea?

PETER. What?

JOANNE. I remember years ago, you know…

PETER. …"in your other life"…

JOANNE. …well, I was in those circles, I would hear things.

PETER. About?

JOANNE. Kerner. There was talk.

PETER. There's always talk.

JOANNE. I'm just saying.

PETER. That was years ago. Look, chances are he'll never hear anything. And if he does, Andy's a smart kid. What could happen?

JOANNE. Aren't you just a little apprehensive?

PETER. Do you hear what you're saying?

JOANNE. I know. You're right. I have papers to grade…

PETER. If he makes the right connections early on…

JOANNE. You're right. God, it's exhausting sometimes.

PETER. What is?

JOANNE. Being enlightened.

Scene Two

(Andy's bedroom. He writes his letter.)

ANDY. "Dear Mr. Kerner, Hi, how are you?" Stupid.

(starting over)

"Dear Mr. Kerner– or whoever screens his mail, Please don't throw this letter away immediately." God, could you be more pathetic?

(starting over)

"Dear Mr. Kerner, I am writing this letter to apologize. You see, I've been stealing from you for years.

(He's pleased, that's a good beginning. **ANDY** *leaves the physical act of writing behind and speaks from the heart.)*

"Let me explain. When I was seven years old, my parents took me to my first Broadway show. It was one of yours, of course. Your revival of *Flash in the Pan*. As corny as it sounds, that matinee changed my life. I still remember staring up at the ceiling of the Majestic Theater and being startled when the overture began, as if I'd finally come home to a place I never knew existed. But it wasn't really an overture, just a sneaky prelude that brought on Molly, our heroine, to stand before the curtain and sing about her dreams of the big city. But it wasn't really a curtain. My heart was pounding as suddenly all the people important to the story seemed to materialize out of thin air. I'd never seen a scrim before.

(The back wall becomes transparent – it too is a scrim. We see **BRADLEY**, **MARTIN KERNER**'s *assistant, going through the day's mail. He opens Andy's letter and reads it.)*

"The effect took my breath away, so much better than in the movies. In the movies, they can show you anything, so what's the point? In the theater, you need guts and know-how to make a moment work. That scrim effect, those characters appearing to deliver their smart and funny lines, to sing their songs, and then disappear with the flick of a dimmer switch, lodged in my sub-conscious immediately.

(**MARTIN KERNER** *enters.* **BRADLEY** *holds out Andy's letter.*)

BRADLEY. I think you should read this.

(**KERNER** *reads.*)

ANDY. "I know, because ever since, I've been dreaming Martin Kerner dreams. Sometimes I can't wait to go to sleep so I can see the latest hit show, directed by the best. 'What does he have up his sleeve tonight?' (Last Tuesday it was two turntables and a ton of dry ice. That dream could run for years.) So you see, I have been stealing from you for a long time. I hope you don't mind.

BRADLEY. Cute, huh?

ANDY. "Anyway, I read in the paper that you're going to mount your musical, *Disraeli* this summer in London. That's one show I know really well. Not only did I see the Broadway production, but I did the show at my high school. I played Ben (in the original keys) and designed the sets. In fact, Mrs. Leach gave me credit in the program as co-director because I was so dedicated. I was also the one who persuaded Mrs. Leach to do it when everyone else wanted to do *Bye Bye Birdie.* That should give you some idea of my determination.

Now, maybe you already have an assistant, but if you don't, it would be an honor to work for you this summer."

KERNER. Ah.

ANDY. "I would be thrilled to do anything, the lowest jobs the theater has to offer, just to be there and see you in action. I know I would learn a tremendous amount. I also know that I am well prepared for such an opportunity, if I do say so myself. I hope to hear from you. But if not, thank you for directing my dreams."

ANDY. *(cont.)* "Sincerely, Andrew Lipman."

*(The lights start to fade on **KERNER** and **BRADLEY**. But then they pop back up.)*

"P.S. Don't be put off by my stationary, 'From the Desk of Andrew Lipman.' It was a Bar-Mitzvah gift three years ago from my Aunt Sedelle. It looks very sophisticated, but I'm still writing under a Snoopy desk lamp. Besides, all my friends call me Andy. As in, 'Can you get us more coffee, Andy? Will you run over to Harrod's, Andy?' Anything you say."

*(**KERNER** hands the letter back to **BRADLEY** as the lights fade. Lights up on **PETER** and **JOANNE** reading the letter themselves.)*

ANDY. *(cont.)* What do you think?

JOANNE. It's too deferential. You don't have to flatter him so much.

PETER. Maybe you don't need the P.S.

ANDY. I have to end on something light so it won't seem like I'm asking for a job. And that's where I put in I'm sixteen and the reference to Harrod's.

PETER. Yeah, I saw that.

ANDY. I want to sound young but worldly.

PETER. It's all you, that's what's important.

JOANNE. I wouldn't kow-tow to him so much.

ANDY. Yeah, well, I would. So, should I send it?

PETER. Send it.

ANDY. Mom?

JOANNE. If you want to, send it.

ANDY. I'm sending it.

(walking off)

It's stupid. He probably won't even write back.

*(**PETER** steps offstage.)*

JOANNE. *(to audience)* He didn't. Andy went off to college.

PETER. *(returning with Joanne's coat)* Harvard. Why don't you say it? He went to Harvard.

JOANNE. He went to Harvard.

PETER. And he wasn't a legacy.

JOANNE. *(indulging him)* He did it on his own.

PETER. You never tell people.

JOANNE. I never get the chance.

> (**PETER** *exits.*)
>
> *(back to audience)* Anyway. Two years later, two years, a letter arrived. Kerner wanted to see him.
>
> (**ANDY** *enters, well-scrubbed and dressed in khaki pants, a jacket and tie.*)

ANDY. How do I look?

JOANNE. Adorable.

ANDY. That's so not what I was going for.

JOANNE. Handsome. You look like a handsome young man with a brilliant future. All right?

ANDY. You don't have to drive me.

JOANNE. I have to go into the city anyway.

ANDY. I can drive myself.

JOANNE. And worry about parking? You're late as it is.

ANDY. I could take the train.

JOANNE. You'll get filthy. Don't be ridiculous.

ANDY. All right. Fine.

JOANNE. Let's go.

ANDY. You're not coming in with me.

JOANNE. I know.

Scene Three

*(Kerner's office/apartment. Pictures of **KERNER** with his famous friends and colleagues cover the walls. **BRADLEY** welcomes a very nervous **ANDY**.)*

ANDY. Hi, I'm Andy Lipman.

BRADLEY. Of course you are. Bradley.

ANDY. Oh, we talked on the phone.

BRADLEY. And it was delightful. It's going to be a few minutes, he's on a call. Have a seat.

ANDY. *(gesturing to the only chair)* Here?

BRADLEY. Go for it. That's a nice tie.

ANDY. Thank you. It's Brooks Brothers.

BRADLEY. Of course it is.

(The phone rings.)

BRADLEY. Excuse me.

(answering the phone)

Martin Kerner's office. Oh, hi, Hal. Yeah, you know, he's here but he's on a call and he's got somebody waiting to have lunch. Are you around this afternoon? Okay. Bye bye.

(hangs up)

Hal Prince.

ANDY. That was my guess. Wow. And you made him wait.

BRADLEY. Just for little ol' you. How about that?

*(**ANDY** smiles, blushes.)*

ANDY. What was he calling about? I mean, it's none of my business...

BRADLEY. I really shouldn't.

ANDY. Right, no, sure. So, what is Mr. Kerner working on these days?

BRADLEY. Too much, as usual. And it's especially crazy right now because of the house.

ANDY. The one in Connecticut? I read that interview in the Arts and Leisure section…

BRADLEY. No, we're renovating a house on Fire Island. It's a nightmare. You can't get anything done out there and, of course, he has to have it finished for the season. Have to keep all the boys happy…

(**ANDY** *fidgets. He's uncomfortable and tries to hide it.*)

ANDY. Oh…well. I hope it all works out.

BRADLEY. Maybe you'll come visit. Plenty of room.

ANDY. Oh, uh, yeah, that would be…great.

(*We hear* **KERNER** *finish his call offstage.*)

KERNER. (*from offstage*) Bradley!

(**KERNER** *enters.* **ANDY** *rises and prepares.*)

Okay, if their lawyers call, tell them we've got to have an answer by Tuesday.

BRADLEY. Hal Prince called. I said you'd call him back.

KERNER. Fine.

(**KERNER** *finally notices* **ANDY**. *He smiles.*)

Well, there he is. You must be Andy. At last we meet.

ANDY. Mr. Kerner, it's such an honor.

KERNER. Oh, please, don't be formal with me. This is great, just great. That's a nice tie.

BRADLEY. It's Brooks Brothers.

KERNER. Of course it is. Your letter was fabulous.

ANDY. Thank you.

KERNER. I understand you don't live there anymore, in… where was it?

ANDY. Port Washington. No, my parents are still on the island. But I'm at school in Boston.

KERNER. Oh, of course. Where?

ANDY. Um, Harvard?

BRADLEY. Where else?

KERNER. Well, no kidding. That's great. Just great. So, I hope you haven't been waiting long.

ANDY. Only two years.

KERNER. I meant just now. But, point taken. I get pretty busy, things get put on the back burner…

BRADLEY. Like my raise.

KERNER. Has he been bothering you?

ANDY. Not at all. He was telling me about your house.

KERNER. House?

ANDY. The one on Fire Island.

(**KERNER** *looks at* **BRADLEY**, *annoyed.*)

KERNER. Bradley must be in a chatty mood. So, you ready for lunch?

ANDY. I'm starved.

KERNER. Me too. Have you ever been to Café des Artistes?

ANDY. No. I've heard of it.

KERNER. It's good. I think you'll like it.

(*to* **BRADLEY**)

They know we're coming?

BRADLEY. You're all set.

KERNER. Let's walk. Is that okay?

ANDY. Sure.

BRADLEY. Have fun.

(**BRADLEY** *exits as the lights change to indicate* **ANDY** *and* **KERNER**'s *walk.*)

ANDY. (*to audience*) And we walked, on a perfect New York day, ten blocks along the park. Me, Andy Lipman, walking down the street with Martin Kerner, giant of the American Theater.

KERNER. How old are you now, Andy?

ANDY. Eighteen.

KERNER. Eighteen. That's great. Just great.

ANDY. It feels okay.

KERNER. You'll find I ask how old you are every once in a while. It's not because I'm forgetful– I admit it, I am– but it helps me figure out where you are and what you need to know.

ANDY. Is there a plan I should be following?

KERNER. Maybe. I had one.

ANDY. Could I have a copy?

KERNER. Here we are.

ANDY. *(to audience)* And with that, he opened the door, ushering me into this "cafe for artists."

(They arrive at the restaurant. A **WAITER** *(played by* **PETER***) greets them.)*

PETER (AS WAITER). Ah, Mr. Kerner. Right this way.

ANDY. *(to audience)* People looked up and whispered to each other. Friends of Kerner's smiled and nodded. I smiled back.

(They sit.)

(to audience) And suddenly, there I was. Face to face with the man whose name I had known my whole life from Original Cast albums and books of Best Plays of the Season.

KERNER. Would you like a little wine?

ANDY. Um, sure, I guess. Yes, thank you.

KERNER. What do you like?

ANDY. Whatever you pick, I'm sure, will be fine.

KERNER. Your mother raised you well. We'll have to get you over that.

ANDY. Right. I...yeah.

*(***KERNER** *reads the wine list.)*

KERNER. Relax. I was exactly the same around your age.

(to the **WAITER***)*

Bring us two glasses of the Montrachet.

PETER (AS WAITER). Very good.

(The **WAITER** *exits.)*

KERNER. But listen. The sooner you can think of me as just a friend, the more useful this can be for you.

ANDY. Okay. Sure. Martin.

KERNER. Marty, if you like.

ANDY. Marty. Okay.

KERNER. You want to loosen your tie? You look like you're choking.

(KERNER helps ANDY loosen his tie a bit.)

That's better, isn't it? Now, just relax.

ANDY. Okay.

(ANDY bounces in his seat and takes a breath. Then his body goes slack and he slumps down like a rag doll, emitting a Jerry Lewis yelp of the "Hey, lady!" variety. KERNER is only mildly amused. ANDY sits back up.)

ANDY. Sorry. Just a little Jerry Lewis bit.

KERNER. I didn't think kids your age liked Jerry Lewis.

ANDY. I don't. I was just being silly. Sorry.

KERNER. Don't be. Interesting thing about Lewis. He's fallen completely out of favor here in the U.S....

ANDY. ...but he's incredibly popular in France. I know. Everybody makes jokes about that.

KERNER. *(a touch of anger)* Maybe they do, but you haven't heard what I have to say about it, have you?

ANDY. No. I'm sorry...

KERNER. Nobody stops and examines why Lewis pleases them. It's simple really. The French have a profound distaste for Americans, bordering on contempt. And Lewis – whom I've dealt with and believe me, it's no picnic – provides them with this pathetic American grotesque, this graceless, ugly buffoon to laugh at. It's really quite disturbing.

ANDY. You're right, I never thought of it that way. I mean, I've never been to France but...

KERNER. Do me a favor. Don't assume you know what I'm going to say. Because I might say something much more interesting than you think. You've got to be open and receptive to me. Otherwise this is a waste of my time and yours. Got it?

ANDY. Yes.

KERNER. Let's order. You ready?

*(**KERNER** smiles as the waiter arrives with the wine. **KERNER** orders silently as **ANDY** again addresses the audience.)*

ANDY. *(to audience)* Yikes! Calm down, Andy. Just breathe. And pay attention.

PETER AS WAITER. Excellent choice.

*(The **WAITER** goes. **KERNER** and **ANDY** clink glasses.)*

KERNER. So. Harvard. God, what I wouldn't give to be going to a school like that, to experience all that for the first time.

ANDY. It's okay, I guess.

KERNER. It'll go by quickly. Use it, every way you can.

ANDY. I'm trying. I've been doing a lot of theater.

KERNER. Great.

ANDY. I've acted in a bunch of shows and I started directing.

KERNER. What was the last show you did?

ANDY. Well, actually, it was one of yours. *By a Thread.*

KERNER. Oh, Jesus, no kidding.

ANDY. I directed and played Sam, the sweatshop union leader.

KERNER. I was a very young man when I wrote that.

ANDY. Yeah, but it still plays. Especially now with Reagan and the whole shift to the Right. What it says about the gap between rich and poor in this country…

KERNER. Yes, I was a good little Leftie.

ANDY. I think it's an awesome play.

KERNER. I wish I'd seen your production.

ANDY. It was okay. I had a little trouble getting the love story to work.

KERNER. So did we. That's where it always fell apart. How did you handle it?

ANDY. I played romantic music underneath the scene on the fire escape. Caruso on an old Victrola coming from Mrs. Sullivan's apartment on the second floor.

KERNER. Interesting. Go on.

ANDY. Sam and Katie are talking about money problems and the shop, and suddenly they stop and listen to this incredible music – that voice, filled with static, and barely audible over the noise from the street. A world of art and beauty is calling to them, promising a richer life. They both hear it. And that's why they fall in love.

(**KERNER** *is impressed and moved.*)

KERNER. Wonderful. I got a chill.

ANDY. It seemed to do the trick.

KERNER. I'll bet. I wish Harold had been that on the ball.

ANDY. Oh, wow…I'm sure Clurman had his good points. I read *On Directing*.

KERNER. What did you think?

ANDY. I liked it.

KERNER. Good!

ANDY. Especially the notes in the back on specific productions.

KERNER. Why don't you do that? Pick some plays you know and write up your thoughts, how you would approach each one. Then send them to me.

ANDY. Cool. An assignment!

KERNER. It'll be a good place for us to start. See where you are, help you develop your own style.

ANDY. I'd love that. Thank you.

KERNER. I gotta tell you, this is so much fun for me. Sitting here with you instead of the same old bunch of phonies.

(**KERNER** *offers a wave to acquaintances at another table.*)

ANDY. Well, any time...

KERNER. You know, they keep asking me to write my autobiography and I think I'm going to give it a shot.

ANDY. Wow, excellent.

KERNER. Looking at you, at the point you're at, and going over the stuff I've done, it helps me focus.

ANDY. Glad to be of help. You can thank me in the acknowledgements.

KERNER. Good idea. I'll have to do that. Remind me.

(The WAITER brings food.)

PETER (AS WAITER). Here we are.

ANDY. *(to audience)* I was doing better. Maybe it was the wine. It was time for me to ask questions.

KERNER. What do you want to know?

ANDY. Everything. Start with the musicals. *Flash in the Pan.*

KERNER. Well, that's an interesting one. I had never done a musical before. I was coming off the moderate success of *The Rocket's Red Glare* but I had nothing new to follow it. The idea came to me in this tiny bar downtown. There was this clumsy waitress with thick horn-rimmed glasses who had just moved to New York, desperate to be a ballerina...

(ANDY turns to the audience as KERNER continues his story inaudibly.)

ANDY. *(to audience)* And the stories began. An endless stream that made my head spin. And the people in them, this was beyond name-dropping. These were his friends, his colleagues. The names didn't drop with a thud, they pierced the air, clear as a bell.

(The WAITER appears holding a glass and strikes it with a spoon: DING. He then does so each time we would hear a famous name.)

ANDY. *(to KERNER)* Tell me about *(DING).*

KERNER. Everybody wants to know about *(DING).*

ANDY. Is she difficult to work with? I hear she's insane.

KERNER. They're all difficult to work with. They're all insane. But I gave *(DING)* her first starring role, opposite *(DING)*.

ANDY. Was that before she married *(DING)*?

KERNER. Please, she was still sleeping with *(DING)*. And *(DING)*.

ANDY. Oh, my God!

KERNER. That was one wild company between *(DING)* chasing *(DING)* and *(DING)* who was a drunk. But *(DING)* had something, even then. In the subway number, she refused to let go of the hand-rail. So, finally, the choreographer…

ANDY. Oh, *(DING)*!

KERNER. Yes, that's right. He and I had to stage the whole number that way, with *(DING)* following *(DING)* from car to car, never letting go. It was everybody's favorite number. What's-his-name, um, um, um… *(DING)* wrote three paragraphs about it in his review.

ANDY. It's a classic.

KERNER. So *(DING)* knew what she had. But she ended up as crazy as *(DING)* who took years off my life. I remember, we were at this party thrown by *(DING)*, with *(DING, DING, DING, DING, DING)* and *(DING)*. And in the middle of charades, *(DING)* threw a drink at *(DING)* because he praised *(DING)* in that other show with *(DING)* and *(DING)*. Don't repeat any of this.

ANDY. *(to audience)* I was in heaven.

*(The **WAITER** takes a bow and exits.)*

KERNER. But I don't like talking this way. I mean, hey, we all love that stuff, that's part of what draws us in the first place. But at some point, if you're an artist, you've got to turn it off so you don't get stuck in that catty, fan mentality bullshit. You've got to know which side of the footlights you're on. Otherwise, you end up with nothing but camp.

ANDY. Right. I hate that.

KERNER. Of course you do. That's why you're sitting here talking to me instead of asking for my autograph. The stories are great but keep them in their proper place. Years from now, you'll have plenty of stories of your own.

ANDY. I hope so. I've always dreamed of a life in the theater. I made my parents throw my tenth birthday party at Sardi's.

KERNER. It's not all dinners at Sardi's, thank God.

ANDY. I know, it's a lot of work. But that's what I want more than anything. To work.

KERNER. Well, this is to help you get there. To give you the tools so you don't have to reinvent the wheel. The "guts and know-how" you wrote about in your letter.

ANDY. You remember...

KERNER. But you have to learn to walk before you can run.

ANDY. That's so true. It's like, at school, there are all these people directing shows for like the first time and they're doing lesbian versions of *Three Sisters*. Or this guy Bruce Radford, this big hot-shit senior who just did *Woyzeck* in the Adams House swimming pool, and I just think, God, wait a second.

KERNER. Right, sure.

ANDY. I mean, these people couldn't direct a decent production of *Our Town* and look what they're doing.

KERNER. Well, not everyone should do *Our Town*. If this guy – what is it?

ANDY. Bruce Radford.

KERNER. If Bruce Radford is doing wild stuff, hey, that's his thing. You should see it for what it is, there could be some value there.

(ANDY regroups.)

ANDY. You're so right.

KERNER. You need the ability to look at what's out there so you can say, "That's good," or, "That's a tub of shit, but I'll take away what I need."

ANDY. I'm too closed. I am. I'll work on that.

KERNER. I know I'm not exactly the king of the avant-garde. My work's in the high middle-brow, that's where I'm comfortable.

ANDY. Me too. I'm not ashamed to love commercial theater.

KERNER. You should be, most of it's shit.

ANDY. Oh, yeah… But when it's good…

KERNER. Exactly! When it's connected, when it's got balls. When it gets you in your head, your heart, and your dick, then bingo. But you gotta have all three.

ANDY. You think I'm leaving one of them out?

KERNER. That's for you to answer. I don't know enough yet. What I do know is this. You're a sensitive, smart kid. You can act, you can direct, you can write. If your development goes the way I hope, I can see you having that kind of career. One like mine, like Mike Nichols…

ANDY. That sounds good.

KERNER. And then, at some point, when we work together, I'll know I can take that stuff for granted. Anything's possible for you. What's most important is that you push out the bullshit and aim for the Truth, capital 'T.' Face it. Really face it, face it all. That's our job, Andy. You understand?

ANDY. Yes.

KERNER. No, you don't. But you've got time. How old are you?

ANDY. Eighteen.

KERNER. Eighteen. That's great. You just promise me. Promise me you'll always remember what led you here. Promise me you'll never forget the sweet, nervous kid in the khaki pants and the Brooks Brothers tie. You promise?

ANDY. I promise.

KERNER. You do that, and you can't miss.

ANDY. *(to the audience)* And suddenly, all I could think of was *Charlie and the Chocolate Factory*.

(**ANDY** *rises. The lights change. Swirls of clouds. Music.*)

It was my favorite story as a kid and when the movie came out, I made my father take me twice. I'll never forget the charge I felt, the strange excitement, seeing Gene Wilder as Willy Wonka, the mad candy manufacturer in his purple velvet frock coat, taking little Charlie Bucket up in the Great Glass Elevator.

(**KERNER** *takes the part of Willy Wonka.*)

KERNER. "How did you like the chocolate factory, Charlie?"

ANDY. *(as Charlie)* "I think it's the most wonderful place in the whole world."

KERNER. "I'm pleased to hear you say that. Because I'm giving it to you. I can't go on forever. And I don't really want to try. That's why I decided I had to find a child. A very honest, loving child, to tell all my most precious candy-making secrets."

ANDY. *(to audience)* I must have been four or five when I saw it, but I can still remember how I felt when Charlie ran into Willy Wonka's arms. This magnificent, exasperating older man who was giving him the keys to his kingdom as they soared through the air in the Great Glass Elevator. Higher and higher as his home became smaller and smaller. I think then there's talk about going to pick up the rest of Charlie's family, but I always ignored that part. What would they do in the chocolate factory? No. Only Charlie could appreciate this incredible gift– his future, handed to him by a magical man who recognized his goodness.

KERNER. "Now, Charlie, don't forget what happened to the man who suddenly got everything he ever wanted."

ANDY. "What happened?"

KERNER. "He lived happily ever after."

(**ANDY** *runs into* **KERNER**'s *arms as the music swells.*)

Scene Four

(**JOANNE** *waits in* **KERNER***'s office with* **BRADLEY**.)

JOANNE. I would have waited outside...

BRADLEY. That's all right.

JOANNE. ...but it got very chilly all of a sudden.

(*looks at pictures on the wall*)

They're very impressive.

BRADLEY. What?

JOANNE. The pictures. With all his famous friends. Incredible. Is this...?

BRADLEY. (*without looking*) Jackie O. Costume party.

JOANNE. He's had quite a life.

BRADLEY. It's still going.

JOANNE. Oh, of course. I didn't mean...Have you been... with him a long time?

BRADLEY. Excuse me?

JOANNE. Working here, for Mr. Kerner.

BRADLEY. A long time.

JOANNE. That's nice. They're certainly having a long lunch. It's three o'clock. I wonder what's keeping them.

BRADLEY. (*aside*) Maybe Andy's still stuck in the sling.

JOANNE. What?

BRADLEY. Nothing.

JOANNE. No. I heard that. That wasn't funny.

BRADLEY. I'm sorry. I didn't think you'd catch it.

JOANNE. Well, I did. It wasn't funny.

(**ANDY** *and* **KERNER** *can be heard offstage.*)

ANDY. ...the first act is perfect but after that...

KERNER. Exactly, it worked with Noel and Gertie because of who they were but...

(*They enter, spot* **JOANNE**.)

ANDY. Mom...

JOANNE. I was waiting outside, but it got chilly…

KERNER. You should have come in right away. We don't want you out in the cold.

ANDY. Martin Kerner, this is my mother, Joanne Lipman.

KERNER. Hello, Joanne. It's a pleasure.

JOANNE. Oh, for me, too. I've seen all your shows. Thank you for taking such an interest in Andy. It means a lot to him.

KERNER. It means a lot to me, too. He's a special kid. You've done a wonderful job.

JOANNE. Oh. Well, thank you. We did our best.

KERNER. It shows.

JOANNE. We've had our rough patches. There were times in school when Andy just coasted along and wouldn't crack the books…

ANDY. Mom!

JOANNE. No, but he's a good kid. We're pretty lucky.

KERNER. I'll say. You don't have to worry about this one.

JOANNE. Yes, I do – he's an only child.

KERNER. You shouldn't say things like that.

JOANNE. I'm sorry?

KERNER. It puts terrible pressure on him.

JOANNE. Oh, I see. I was joking, really…

KERNER. Even so. I can tell just from meeting him today that Andy feels the weight of your expectations. Now that's fine up to a point. But then it could become destructive.

JOANNE. *(Who does he think he is?)* And I am sensitive to that, believe me…

ANDY. We should probably go.

JOANNE. I work every day as a high school English Teacher, so I've seen what happens when parents push their children too hard. I drove forty minutes every morning to a different district just so my son wouldn't have his mother embarrassing him in the hallway. I am scrupulous in what I say, what I do…

KERNER. Ah, yes, well, then you understand perfectly. Forgive me, I don't mean to interfere. Certain things just get me going.

JOANNE. Me too.

ANDY. Okay, we'll get out of your hair…

BRADLEY. Oh, wait, Andy, let me give you the info where we'll be the next few weeks.

ANDY. Thanks.

(**BRADLEY** *starts writing out information for* **ANDY** *who is desperate to leave.*)

BRADLEY. If all else fails, you can always leave a message here and I'll hook you up with Marty. I'm sort of the gate-keeper. Where's that itinerary?

(**BRADLEY** *looks for it as* **KERNER** *and* **JOANNE** *continue.*)

KERNER. I can see where Andy gets his artistic temperament.

JOANNE. Can you?

KERNER. Oh, yes.

JOANNE. His father is an architect.

KERNER. And you, an English teacher. With a passion for the great books.

JOANNE. I suppose so. And, truth be told, I was a dancer years ago.

ANDY. Oh, God. *(to* **BRADLEY***)* Are you done?

BRADLEY. Just a sec.

KERNER. No kidding?

JOANNE. Here in the city. Back "in my other life."

KERNER. Why do you say that? We only have one life. This is it.

JOANNE. That's true. It just feels…I don't know. Actually, I auditioned for you.

KERNER. For me? Really?

JOANNE. For the ensemble in *Love All Around.* I was so excited. I wanted so badly for you to notice me. I wore this bright purple outfit and sang as loudly as I could. But I wasn't what you were looking for. Too tall. Or something. It was my last audition. Ever.

KERNER. I'm sorry.

JOANNE. Oh, that's all right. Things worked out.

ANDY. I'm ready to go. Can we go now?

JOANNE. I'm waiting for you. Goodbye.

BRADLEY. So long. Bye, Andy.

ANDY. See 'ya. Goodbye…Marty.

KERNER. Come here.

>*(**KERNER** gives **ANDY** a hug. **JOANNE** watches, uncomfortable.)*

Keep up the good work. Send me those ideas.

ANDY. I will.

>*(**ANDY** and **JOANNE** start to leave when **KERNER** stops them.)*

KERNER. Wait a minute. Purple? Bright purple?

JOANNE. With a red kerchief. It was hideous.

KERNER. You know, I remember you. I do. You're right, you weren't what we were looking for but you were very good. If I remember correctly, we all talked about you for quite some time. You were terrific.

JOANNE. I will choose to believe you.

KERNER. Good.

>*(to **ANDY**)*

I hope you will, too.

ANDY. I believe you. Every word.

>*(**KERNER** smiles and waves them off.)*

KERNER. All right, get out of here.

>*(**ANDY** and **JOANNE** exit.)*

BRADLEY. You don't really remember, do you?

KERNER. No. But wouldn't it say lovely things about both of us if I did?

BRADLEY. What do you think?

KERNER. Too early to tell. But there's something there. He's got the smarts, the vulnerability…God, if you could bottle that…Always fun to be around.

BRADLEY. I hope you'll be gentle with him.

KERNER. What does that mean?

BRADLEY. He's listening to you, "every word."

KERNER. What are you worried about?

BRADLEY. I just have a feeling about him.

KERNER. Truth. Jealous?

BRADLEY. Of course.

KERNER. Well, I appreciate your concern. Duly noted. Very sweet.

*(***KERNER** *kisses* **BRADLEY** *on the cheek and starts to exit.)*

BRADLEY. He certainly is a cutie.

KERNER. Don't say that.

BRADLEY. Sorry.

KERNER. It's true. But don't say it.

Scene Five

(JOANNE *and* ANDY *arrive at home.* PETER *greets them.*)

PETER. So? What happened? How'd it go?
ANDY. Fine.
JOANNE. He's mad at me. He didn't say a word in the car.
PETER. What did you do?
ANDY. She was there, in his apartment when we got back.
JOANNE. It was cold.
PETER. It was cold. You didn't want her out in the cold.
ANDY. She told him she was a dancer.
PETER. You didn't tell him the purple story, did you?
JOANNE. We were talking…
PETER. Oh, Joanne.
JOANNE. Fine, I'm terrible.
ANDY. I'm not mad. I mean, I could be, but I will not allow anything to ruin this day.
PETER. That good, huh? So, tell us.
ANDY. I don't want to talk about it.
PETER. Come on, that's not fair. What did he say when you met?
ANDY. I don't know. He laughed a lot.
PETER. He thought you were funny.
ANDY. Yeah. Oh, and I think he was impressed when he found out I'm at Harvard.
PETER. He didn't know?
ANDY. How would he know?
JOANNE. He must not have seen the ad.
ANDY. But it was like I've made good. Like he was right to get in touch with me.
PETER. Did he say anything about why it took two years?
ANDY. Not really. He's busy. So, anyway, then we went to lunch.

PETER. Where'd he take you?

ANDY. Café des Artistes.

PETER. Very nice. I go there with clients.

ANDY. It was beautiful.

JOANNE. I've never been.

PETER. Oh, it's excellent. I'll take you sometime.

JOANNE. *(doubtful)* Sure.

PETER. *(to ANDY)* What'd you have and what'd he have?

ANDY. Dad...!

PETER. What? Okay. So then what did you talk about?

ANDY. I don't know. The theater. Life. He said something about working together.

PETER. Really? No kidding.

JOANNE. He can be very charming.

ANDY. What's that supposed to mean?

JOANNE. Nothing. I said he was charming.

ANDY. Yeah, but you said it like I'm being naïve or something. He said we might work together. He did.

JOANNE. All right, okay. I believe you. I wasn't there.

ANDY. No, you were waiting at the apartment.

PETER. Hey, Andy, lay off. So, he wants to help you. That's terrific. A guy like that could pull some strings and who knows? Did he say when?

ANDY. It wasn't like that. But he said I'm smart, that I can act, I can direct, and write, and if all goes well...

JOANNE. How does he know?

ANDY. What?

JOANNE. How does he know what you can do? He's never seen you.

ANDY. No, but...from my letter, from how I talk and think. He sees something in me.

PETER. Of course. Why wouldn't he?

ANDY. As hard as that may be for you to believe...

JOANNE. We know what you can do. We've seen every play, every concert...

PETER. So, then what?

ANDY. We were there. Just talking, like equals. Well, not equals, but as if he valued my opinion. And whatever I said, he would take it and build on it. He knows so much! Just sitting there, I was…enriched.

PETER. That's fantastic.

ANDY. You don't know what it's like. To have someone like that believe in you.

JOANNE. We believe in you.

(ANDY knows he's said something hurtful. He tries to make it right.)

ANDY. You know what I mean.

PETER. Sure.

ANDY. Somebody famous, who's been there…

PETER. It's fine.

JOANNE. Go up and get changed. I don't want to have that stuff dry-cleaned if I can help it.

(ANDY kisses JOANNE on the cheek.)

ANDY. Thanks for driving me.

(ANDY exits.)

PETER. Well, that could be good.

(beat)

What?

JOANNE. Did you see the look on his face?

PETER. He's excited. It was a big day.

JOANNE. It's more than that. I've seen that look before. At school. Those eyes that say, "You are opening new worlds to me. You are here to help me understand myself and I am bright enough to let you."

PETER. That must be gratifying.

JOANNE. It was. It was the greatest. But I don't get that look anymore. The kids are jaded, or I'm too old…

PETER. No, you're not.

JOANNE. Last week, there I was for the hundredth time, teaching *Madame Bovary*, doing my usual spiel about romance and longing to escape a boring life.

PETER. Sounds good.

JOANNE. "All right," I said. "Okay. Why does Emma marry Charles in the first place? All right, who wants to give it a shot? Anybody? All right. Okay?" And then I realized they weren't listening. They were laughing. At me. In hysterics.

PETER. Why?

JOANNE. I say that – "All right. Okay." I say that a lot. One of them, Jordan – a smart one, I just gave him an 'A' – he picked up on it and told the others. They were counting how many times I said those words. "All right. Okay." Keeping score. Making a fool of me.

PETER. Kids are cruel, you know that.

JOANNE. Jordan marked down eighty-three times in forty minutes.

PETER. It's just a verbal tic.

JOANNE. No, I'm stalling. Covering as my mind wanders, wondering how I used to pull this off. I'm not the "cool teacher" anymore. I'm not their "friend." They'd rather be in Miss Nelson's class – pretty little Marsha, who lets them call her by her first name while they analyze Bruce Springsteen lyrics as "the poetry of our age." They love her. I'm just another burnt-out fool with tenure.

PETER. Stop it.

JOANNE. Peter, it's all right.

(catching herself)

It's "okay." I haven't given up. Yet. But I started to believe I'd never see that look on a kid's face again. And now I have. And it's not for me.

(She rises.)

I have papers to grade.

(She exits. **PETER** *watches after her.)*

Scene Six

(Andy's room. **ANDY** *reads.* **PETER** *knocks in the doorway.)*

PETER. What shuttle do you want to take back tomorrow?
ANDY. Eleven? I have Troilus rehearsal.
PETER. So, you had a good time today.
ANDY. Yeah.
PETER. I'm glad.

*(***PETER*** *almost exits but then turns back to share his own story.)*

PETER. You know, I had something similar. When I was in school, this famous architect, a hero of mine, came for a symposium. I was so excited, I tried to ask the perfect questions, to impress him without being a brown-nose…You know the act…

ANDY. Did he notice you?

PETER. He took me to lunch. Then he offered me a job, to join his new firm out West. They were doing this Neo-Bauhaus, Pre-Post-Modern stuff – the ugly buildings we all hate today, but back then…He wanted me to leave school right away, so I would never get my degree.

ANDY. I bet Grandma loved that.

PETER. Oh, boy. And I was dating your mother, so she had her career to think about. That was back…

ANDY. …"in her other life."

PETER. It just seemed a little too risky. So I told him no.

ANDY. Couldn't you finish school and then go?

PETER. He said he couldn't wait. Or wouldn't, I don't know. He was very gracious about it. But a month or so later, he was back in town and we arranged to have lunch, and I showed up late. Ten minutes, tops. Well, he laid into me like you wouldn't believe. "Just who the fuck do you think you are? After what I've done for you! This is how you repay me, you worthless sycophant!"

In front of everybody. I was just a kid, and the traffic that day was the worst...

(beat)

PETER. Just be careful.

ANDY. Thanks.

PETER. You having fun at school?

ANDY. Yeah.

PETER. I know you're worried about grades and your theater things, but don't forget to have fun. Don't forget to date and stuff like that.

ANDY. I'm okay.

PETER. What happened with that girl we heard about?

ANDY. Karen? We're just friends.

PETER. Well...you've got plenty of schools up there to choose from. In my day, they used to say Wellesley had the best looking girls.

ANDY. Times change.

PETER. Yeah, I guess they do.

ANDY. Dad, I'm fine.

PETER. Just checking.

*(He kisses **ANDY** on the head.)*

See you tomorrow.

ANDY. Dad? Do you ever wish you had gone with him?

PETER. Sure.

Scene Seven

(A phone rings. **KERNER** *calls from a hotel.* **ANDY** *answers in his dorm room.)*

ANDY. Hello?

KERNER. Andy. It's Marty.

ANDY. Oh, God. Hi!

KERNER. I hope it's not too late.

ANDY. No, I'm up studying.

KERNER. Past midnight?

ANDY. And watching Letterman and eating pizza. Where are you?

KERNER. L.A. They're showing a restored print of *Divertimento.*

ANDY. Did I ever tell you how much I love that movie?

KERNER. It looks good, I was surprised. It's still a bit too theatrical.

ANDY. That's why I like it. I don't know how you managed to direct a good movie within the system. I'm never going to work in Hollywood.

KERNER. Never say "never," kid. It'll bite you in the ass.

ANDY. Right. But you hear all these stories – everyone's so plastic and greedy…

KERNER. Never say "everyone." There are some good people out here.

ANDY. Right, that's a generalization. I'm sure there are wonderful things about the city…

KERNER. It's a fucking wasteland. So, Bradley gave me your last few letters.

*(***KERNER*** goes through a small pile of letters from* **ANDY.***)*

ANDY. Oh, yeah, well, you said I should keep you up-to-date…

KERNER. How was *My Fair Lady?*

ANDY. Amazing. We sold out and I got really good reviews.

KERNER. Hey, what did I tell you about –

ANDY. I know, reviews don't matter. But it's nice when they don't kill you.

KERNER. True.

ANDY. Anyway, it went great. I mean, it was pretty small scale, the cast was seven people.

KERNER. You did *My Fair Lady* with seven people?

ANDY. It cut down on the spectacle.

KERNER. I would think so.

ANDY. One girl doubled as Mrs. Higgins and Mrs. Pierce, which was interesting.

KERNER. His mother/his maid, sure.

ANDY. It worked pretty well. Obviously, I'm too young for Higgins, but I think I got a good piece of it.

KERNER. I'm sure you did.

ANDY. There were some things I didn't crack. Like the happy ending, you know, when Eliza comes back, still felt a little dishonest.

KERNER. That's because it is. Higgins doesn't have those feelings and you're sensitive to that.

ANDY. Yeah. Hmm.

KERNER. I went through your production notes.

(KERNER skims the letters.)

ANDY. "My assignment." How'd I do?

KERNER. I'm not here to judge, just to nudge you in the right direction.

ANDY. Right. So how'd I do?

KERNER. Very well. The Marxist *Pajama Game* is intriguing.

ANDY. I thought you'd like that one.

KERNER. But, you know, you're still working from the outside.

ANDY. Oh… what…?

KERNER. You're so concerned with scenic effects– walls flying, scrims, turntables. First of all, you may never get them.

ANDY. Right, I know. But I figured this was hypothetical…

KERNER. I understand that. Nevertheless, you're still paying more attention to how everything looks than to what it all means. For example, take the scrim…

ANDY. My favorite.

KERNER. Exactly. What is a scrim? It's something we use to hide what's really there. To mask. Conceal. It only makes its effect when we throw some light behind it, when we show what's really going on. I don't want you hiding anything.

(Beat.)

You're very quiet.

ANDY. I don't know what to say.

KERNER. Good. Maybe we're getting somewhere.

ANDY. I think we are.

KERNER. I hope so.

ANDY. Oh, Marty, I almost forgot – I started writing this play. I was sort of wondering…

KERNER. I'd love to read it when you have something. I'd be honored.

ANDY. So would I.

KERNER. I should let you get back to your studying and your pizza. Keep up the good work…

ANDY. Thank you so much for calling. I miss you.

KERNER. I miss you, too. You give me such a kick. I know sometimes my yakking at you doesn't make complete sense yet. That's okay. I just want to make sure you keep growing, that you're taking it all in. How old are you now?

ANDY. Nineteen.

KERNER. Nineteen. That's fantastic. Well, know that I'm thinking about you.

ANDY. I'll be home for the holidays.

KERNER. Terrific. Send Bradley the dates. Maybe we'll get together.

*(Lights out on **KERNER** and **ANDY**'s dorm room. **ANDY** addresses the audience.)*

ANDY. *(to audience)* We almost never did. We'd come close from time to time…

*(**BRADLEY** appears and talks to **ANDY** by phone.)*

BRADLEY. He might have time this afternoon. Where are you going to be?

ANDY. I was thinking of taking in a matinee. But I can skip it…

BRADLEY. No, no, you go about your business. Do me a favor – you know what you're going to see?

ANDY. No, I was going to try the half-priced booth…

BRADLEY. Fine, tell you what – call me when you know and what time it lets out. Then we'll go from there. Dinner might be possible depending on three other things that could fall out.

*(Lights out on **BRADLEY**.)*

ANDY. They never did.

*(**JOANNE** and **PETER** enter. **JOANNE** brings a winter coat for **ANDY**.)*

JOANNE. It's disgusting, the way he gets your hopes up.

PETER. The nerve of him. He hasn't even found you a summer job. Next time, say you're too busy to see him.

(They exit.)

ANDY. *(to audience)* But I didn't mind. I enjoyed wandering the city, browsing at Tower Records between my strategically timed phone-calls to headquarters.

*(Lights up again on **BRADLEY** for another phone call.)*

ANDY. Hey, it's Andy.

BRADLEY. Where are you?

ANDY. The corner of 50th and Broadway.

BRADLEY. Hold on.

ANDY. *(to audience)* I felt like a spy.

BRADLEY. Can you meet Marty at the stage door of the St. James in half an hour? He'll be in between meetings but he'd love to see you. It'll only be a few minutes, so it's kind of silly...

ANDY. I'll be there.

(The scene shifts to 44th Street. **KERNER** *comes out a stage door.)*

KERNER. There he is!

ANDY. Hi.

*(***KERNER** *gives him a quick hug.)*

KERNER. Thanks for coming to see me. Sorry this is so brief, I've got this meeting above the Minskoff.

ANDY. I just wanted to say hello.

KERNER. You look great. Just great. It means so much to me, to see you haven't changed. So, what's the latest?

(They walk as they talk.)

ANDY. Well, I'm twenty.

KERNER. I didn't even ask.

ANDY. I figured I'd save you the trouble.

KERNER. I appreciate that. Twenty. Okay.

ANDY. I feel like I'm getting up there, you know?

KERNER. Don't be ridiculous.

ANDY. Yeah, I know, I'm still a kid. But, real life is just around the corner. I keep worrying, like, how am I going to make something of myself that's real?

(They stop walking.)

KERNER. Go on.

ANDY. I'm confused. And I feel like you can help me.

KERNER. Yes. Talk to me.

ANDY. Maybe if I had some idea of opportunities, a job...

KERNER. Oh.

ANDY. Somewhere I could get coffee or answer phones, anything, as long as I got in the door.

KERNER. Well, let me think about it. There are people at some of the regionals I could talk to about you. There's very exciting stuff going on at the regionals.

ANDY. I would appreciate that so much.

KERNER. The jobs will come. That's not what I worry about with you.

ANDY. I'm not sure what you…

KERNER. Be patient. You're young. It will be many years before you realize just how young you are right now. Everything is possible…

(A crusty older agent, **FLORENCE** *(played by* **JOANNE***) approaches.)*

JOANNE (AS FLORENCE). What the hell happened to you?

KERNER. Florence! Jesus, how are you?

JOANNE (AS FLORENCE). I never see you, I never hear from you.

(to **ANDY***)*

We've known each other thirty years. Can you imagine?

KERNER. We met as infants. Florence Green, legendary agent, Andrew Lipman, legend to be. Remember the name, Florence. This one's going to show us all.

JOANNE (AS FLORENCE). Well, you would know.

(to **ANDY***)*

Nice to meet you.

ANDY. Hi.

JOANNE (AS FLORENCE). *(to* **KERNER***)* So, how's everything? Good? Tim?

KERNER. Terrific. You?

JOANNE (AS FLORENCE). Can't complain. But that never stopped me. What are you doing here? You got something going?

KERNER. It's a secret.

JOANNE (AS FLORENCE). You and your secrets. Call me. *(to* **ANDY***)* I'll be looking out for you. Wonderful! New young people in the theater!

(She raises a fist in salute as she walks off.)

ANDY. Thank you for saying that.

KERNER. I meant it.

ANDY. I wish I was that confident.

KERNER. Oh, shit, here we are.

(They stop at the door. **KERNER** *presses a buzzer.)*

ANDY. What are all these meetings about? Can you tell me?

KERNER. A new musical. The working title is *Mad As Hell* but I think we'll change it.

ANDY. *Mad as Hell?* It's not based on *Network*, is it?

KERNER. You got it.

ANDY. Wow. It's a great movie. But…wow.

KERNER. It's a tough one.

*(***KERNER** *presses the door buzzer again.)*

ANDY. You've got all those speeches, and it's so dark. And the love story, if you can call it that, is so scary…

KERNER. I'll go tell them it's off.

ANDY. No! I was just thinking aloud…

KERNER. I'm pretty sure it can work. But it has to be fresh, really plugged in to what's happening now.

ANDY. Well, if anyone can pull it off, it's you. I can't wait to see it, I know that movie so well.

KERNER. Good, I'll need your help. I have my doubts, a friend talked me into it, but the money's in place, so…

(A click indicates the door is now unlocked. **KERNER** *opens it.)*

Keep up the good work.

ANDY. Whatever that is.

KERNER. I'll think about that other stuff. And, hey, I'll bring you in to help me on this.

ANDY. Great.

KERNER. See you soon.

*(***KERNER** *exits.)*

ANDY. *(to audience)* I tried not to expect too much. I really did.

Scene Eight

(ANDY enters with his parents. He's just come home from school for his Christmas vacation.)

PETER. But what exactly is it?

ANDY. It's a show, an original musical, written and performed by students but with a professional director, choreographer, designers...it's very cool. The budget's huge.

PETER. No kidding. I'd always heard of the Hasty Pudding but I never knew...

JOANNE. They're known for something else, right? There's something about the show that's unusual, isn't there?

ANDY. What? That it's all guys?

JOANNE. That's it.

PETER. It's all guys?

ANDY. Onstage. But women can do anything backstage or in the pit.

JOANNE. How nice for them.

ANDY. But the cast is all guys – half as men, half as women. Until the kick line.

PETER. Kick line?

ANDY. The show always ends with a kick line. And everybody's a woman in that, even the guys who play guys.

PETER. And you're...?

ANDY. This year's show takes place in Japan. It's called *Shogun's Heroes*. I got cast as Geisha Had-to-be-there. It's borderline offensive but that's part of the fun. In the kick line, we're all Playboy Bunnies.

JOANNE. And that's only "borderline offensive."

ANDY. If you have a sense of humor.

PETER. No, it sounds funny. It does.

ANDY. You don't have to come. If it offends your sensibilities, or you don't want to see me with breasts, fine. But I'm doing it. The opening's at the end of February, it's black-tie. But forget it.

JOANNE. We'll be there.

PETER. We wouldn't miss it. You kidding me?

ANDY. It's very professional.

PETER. You inviting what's-his-name?

ANDY. Who?

PETER. Kerner.

ANDY. I'll send him something, I always do. Don't worry, he won't show up.

(**ANDY** *exits.* **PETER** *and* **JOANNE** *stare at each other.*)

PETER. Just what I need.

JOANNE. Well… Liberal Arts.

(Lights out on them. **BRADLEY** *appears.)*

BRADLEY. *(speaking a note to Andy)*

"Dear Andy, We got your note about the show. Believe it or not, Marty has to be in Boston that week to accept the Elliot Norton Lifetime Achievement Award. And he's decided to come up a day early just to see you. So, if you could please reserve two tickets for the opening, we'll be there. Break a leg. But don't fall off your heels. Bradley."

(Lights up briefly on **ANDY** *wearing an exaggerated, outrageous get-up as a Japanese Geisha.)*

ANDY. Oh, God.

Scene Nine

*(The crowded lobby of the Hasty Pudding Theater in Cambridge on opening night. **JOANNE**, in a smart outfit, and **PETER**, in black tie, enter and look around.)*

JOANNE. This is thrilling, isn't it?

PETER. Yeah, if only my son weren't dressed as a Japanese hooker.

JOANNE. God, I miss this.

PETER. I know.

JOANNE. Look, there he is. Kerner.

*(**KERNER** appears with **BRADLEY**, dressed in a suit.)*

PETER. He couldn't find a tux?

JOANNE. We should say hello.

PETER. Are you sure?

JOANNE. *(charging ahead)* Mr. Kerner? Hi. It's Joanne Lipman, Andy's mother.

KERNER. Oh, yes, hello. Nice to see you.

JOANNE. This is my husband, Peter.

PETER. It's a pleasure. My son thinks you're the greatest.

KERNER. Oh, well, that's very kind. He's a terrific young man and that's no doubt because of his upbringing.

PETER. *(to **JOANNE**)* You're right. He is charming.

JOANNE. It's so nice of you to come. This will be your first time seeing Andy perform, won't it?

KERNER. Yes, I suppose so.

JOANNE. We've been to everything he's ever done. We're always driving up here to see something.

KERNER. I envy both of you.

PETER. You didn't have to sit through *Troilus and Cressida*. At least he was a man in that.

(an awkward beat)

JOANNE. Andy told us you're here to accept an award.

KERNER. Tomorrow night. It's a Lifetime Achievement Award which is a bit depressing. I'm afraid they'll hand me a placque that says, "That's enough, you're finished."

PETER. I doubt that.

JOANNE. It sounds like a great honor.

KERNER. Well, it's a reminder to get cracking on what I have left to do. And to help those coming up.

PETER. Like Andy.

KERNER. Oh, you don't have to worry about him.

PETER. Really? I mean, I know he's talented, believe me. He's a genius as far as I'm concerned, but to hear it from you, it's like the Good Housekeeping Seal of Approval.

KERNER. I don't pretend to have that kind of authority.

(The lights flash. **KERNER** *begins to move to his seat.* **PETER** *stops him.)*

PETER. No, but still…So, do you think you might be able to help him along? Working for you on a show or something?

KERNER. Well, let him graduate and then he'll take a look around…

PETER. Because I know he has such respect for you. And certainly nobody could help him the way you could in what he loves…

JOANNE. Peter…we'll see.

PETER. I'm getting the not-so-subtle-signal to shut up. I talk too much sometimes because I'm so proud of him. I'll bet your parents were the same way.

KERNER. It's uncanny.

(The lights dim. Two pairs of theater seats appear facing downstage. **JOANNE** *and* **PETER** *sit on one side,* **KERNER** *and* **BRADLEY** *on the other. Background music, laughter, lights to indicate the show they're watching.)*

JOANNE. *(to audience) Shogun's Heroes.* Not my cup of tea but it was cute if you took it in the right spirit – and managed to forget every feminist idea you ever had. It reminded me of Gilbert and Sullivan, which always seems more fun to do than to watch. But the boys were having a wonderful time. And so was the audience, which was plastered long before the curtain rose. They loved Andy, who got every laugh, a real pro. By the time he sang his big solo, Peter and I were holding hands, nervous for him but practically levitating with pride.

(JOANNE and PETER beam. She looks to KERNER.)

(to audience)

Kerner didn't crack a smile.

(The show is over. Applause. We're back in the lobby. ANDY enters in a tuxedo, his hair slicked back. He goes to his parents first. They hug and fuss over him.)

ANDY. Hi. Did you like it?

JOANNE. It was terrific! What did you do to your hair?

ANDY. This is easier after the wig…Dad? How are you doing? Are you okay?

PETER. What, I'm fine. But let me tell you one thing.

ANDY. What?

PETER. You make one ugly Playboy bunny.

ANDY. Well, that's a relief, I guess.

PETER. You're telling me. And let me tell you something else…*(confidentially)*…you were the best. They all looked like amateurs next to you.

ANDY. Yeah, yeah, yeah, fine. So, it's okay?

JOANNE. It's wonderful. Your friend's over there.

(ANDY looks over nervously at KERNER and BRADLEY.)

ANDY. Give me a minute.

(ANDY approaches KERNER and BRADLEY, smiling, embarrassed.)

I wish this wasn't the first thing you saw me do…

BRADLEY. Please, I had a blast.

ANDY. I was so nervous about you coming.

KERNER. Why?

ANDY. I was afraid you'd think I wasn't any good.

KERNER. Oh.

ANDY. And love-sick Geisha girl isn't really my casting.

BRADLEY. I'm not so sure.

KERNER. Bradley, what did you do with the coats?

(BRADLEY exits.)

ANDY. Thanks for coming.

KERNER. What the hell are you doing?

ANDY. What do you mean?

KERNER. You've got all this talent, all these gifts, and you're pissing it all away.

(ANDY is devastated. He tries hard to keep his emotions in check.)

ANDY. You didn't think I was good.

KERNER. Did I say that?

ANDY. No.

KERNER. You were good. That makes it worse. How old are you now?

ANDY. Twenty. I'm still twenty.

KERNER. You're twenty years old. You're educated, you've got all this stuff going on inside you and this is how you spend your time? You're fucking up. This is glib bullshit. It's camp. I thought you were really working on yourself, preparing…

ANDY. I am. Look, I know what this is, I'm not stupid. But this isn't all I do…

KERNER. Well, this is what I see. Maybe if we could really talk to each other as adults, I'd know better, but you're still not ready for that.

ANDY. I'm ready…

KERNER. No, you're not. And, Andy, if I'm wrong, and you're really making the most of what you've got here, then look me in the eye and say, "Fuck you, Marty, you don't know shit. I'm working my balls off." Can you say that to me?

(**ANDY** *is silent, on the verge of tears.*)

I didn't think so. Go ahead, hate me. I know, I'm a bastard. But if I didn't tell you the truth, capital 'T,' I couldn't look myself in the mirror. And I wouldn't be your friend.

ANDY. Thank you. For being honest with me.

(**BRADLEY** *returns and helps* **KERNER** *with his coat.*)

KERNER. You're welcome.

ANDY. Can you still come upstairs to the party?

KERNER. No.

ANDY. The guys would love to meet you.

KERNER. I'm sorry.

ANDY. Well, maybe you can come by tomorrow night after your banquet. There's someone I'd like you to meet...

KERNER. What is this? What are you doing?

ANDY. What?

KERNER. I'm not some performing monkey you can show off to your friends.

ANDY. Of course not.

KERNER. Then don't treat me that way. I've given you a lot of time and attention. Don't make me regret that. I'm tired. You think about what I said.

(**KERNER** *and* **BRADLEY** *exit.* **JOANNE** *and* **PETER** *approach* **ANDY.**)

JOANNE. Okay, where's that opening night party? I want to dance with the leading man.

ANDY. He didn't like it.

PETER. Jerk. What does he know?

ANDY. He says I'm fucking up.

JOANNE. What? How dare he say that tonight!

PETER. It's not nice, it really isn't.

JOANNE. He's just jealous. Because you're young and he's getting Lifetime Achievement awards.

ANDY. He's right.

JOANNE. No, he isn't.

ANDY. Yes, he is! God! I've wasted so much time!

PETER. What nonsense. You're twenty years old. You're at Harvard for chrissake.

ANDY. And I'm coasting along.

PETER. You don't get here by coasting.

ANDY. I did. And he's the only person with the guts to tell me. He's the only one who understands.

PETER. Oh, really. Then what are we? The stupid parents you have to overcome, is that it?

JOANNE. Peter, leave it alone.

PETER. I'm getting pretty tired of this. He idolizes Kerner who barely gives him the time of day – and when he does, he insults him – while we're the ones supporting him, dealing with his problems...

ANDY. You don't deal with my problems.

PETER. What? We don't...

ANDY. No. Because I don't bring them to you. I have problems you don't know anything about.

PETER. Oh, your problems. Like how will I get tickets to the next Broadway show. People dream of having your problems.

ANDY. You're such an asshole.

PETER. What'd you just say to me?

JOANNE. Andy, what is it? Drugs? Is it drugs?

ANDY. No, it's not drugs.

PETER. Who do you share these great problems with?

JOANNE. Andy, tell me. Have you tried to commit suicide? Answer me. Have you tried to commit suicide?

ANDY. I have to go to the party. Leave me alone.

(ANDY exits.)

PETER. Let's go.

JOANNE. We can't leave him like this.

PETER. I'm not going to fight for his approval.

JOANNE. He's got a problem.

PETER. I heard.

JOANNE. We know what it is.

(Beat. So there it is.)

PETER. Has he told you? Has he said something to you?

JOANNE. No. But…

PETER. Then we don't know.

JOANNE. Peter. We're not stupid.

PETER. Until he says something, we don't know.

Scene Ten

(Kerner's Boston hotel suite. There's banging on the door. **KERNER** *enters in a bathrobe and opens the door for* **ANDY** *who enters in a frenzy. He still wears his tuxedo but the tie is gone and his hair is mussed. He's been drinking.)*

ANDY. Thank you for letting me up. They looked at me funny at the front desk.

KERNER. Never mind that.

ANDY. You said something about an adult conversation. Maybe this will be it.

KERNER. Okay, I'm here. Talk to me.

ANDY. I had a fight with my parents.

KERNER. It happens.

ANDY. I was a shit. And they love me so much.

KERNER. Yes, they do.

ANDY. But they don't really know me. I thought I was so close to them, I wanted to be just like them forever, but now…the most important thing has happened and I can't even tell them.

KERNER. Then tell me.

(It takes a moment for **ANDY** *to summon the courage to speak.)*

ANDY. There's this guy. His name is Randy. I know, it's a stupid name, but what can you do? He's younger than I am, a freshman. He's blonde and he's from the South. Oh, I have a picture.

*(***ANDY*** takes a picture out of his wallet and hands it to* **KERNER.** **KERNER** *holds the photo at a slight distance to see it more clearly.)*

KERNER. He looks very sweet.

ANDY. That's who I wanted you to meet.

KERNER. I didn't know.

ANDY. He's not the first guy I've...I mean, I've messed around – cast parties, drunk...it happened and I thought, okay, that was that. But this is different.

KERNER. How is it different?

ANDY. We just...we kept spending time together, listening to cast albums – he'd never heard *Company* before! And we'd always sort of hug goodbye. Then, before Christmas vacation, he came to my room to bring me a card. He handed it to me with this terrified expression, like it was a letter bomb or something. I sat on my bed to read it and the next thing I knew, he was sitting in the corner, all scrunched up on the floor, with his jacket over his head. It was weird.

KERNER. I'll bet.

ANDY. In the card, he said he loved me. He didn't know what this was, what was happening between us. But he loved me. He was afraid I wouldn't want to be his friend anymore.

KERNER. Go on.

ANDY. I walked over to him and I got down on the floor, he was still shaking, and I pulled the jacket off his head...

KERNER. And?

ANDY. We looked at each other. We didn't have to say anything. It was the most wonderful, painful moment of my life. For the first time, I felt completely free. And doomed. Ever since then, I can't think of anything else.

KERNER. Of course.

ANDY. We spend our time running from classes, desperate to see each other...stealing afternoon naps, holding each other in our Brooks Brothers sweaters...sneaking past sleeping roommates as if they don't know, which is pretty ridiculous. I am so...happy.

KERNER. I know.

ANDY. And I don't know what to do. I thought I knew what I was going to be. Now I don't. I've seen the whole gay thing, I've been to piano bars, and that's not me.

KERNER. No.

ANDY. And when I play the good boy for my parents, that's not me either.

KERNER. No.

ANDY. So how do I go on? Help me. What am I going to do?

KERNER. You'll do what you have to. And it will be fine. I'm so proud of you.

(taking ANDY's hand)

You're a man now. This changes everything.

End of Act One.

ACT TWO

Scene One

(Where we left off. **KERNER** *holds* **ANDY**'s *hand. Pause.)*
KERNER. My hand is making you uncomfortable, isn't it?
ANDY. No, it's fine…
KERNER. That's all right. Just relax.
*(***KERNER*** removes* **ANDY**'s *jacket and rubs his shoulders.)*
How are you doing?
ANDY. I'm okay.
KERNER. Good. Now I want you to listen to me. I'm going to tell you what I know. You've done the most important thing in the world. You've made the connection between who you are and how you love. That's a tough thing to do, it takes balls. Especially for someone who wants to be a "good boy." I know you're afraid. I know there's stuff to think about. But don't let any of that stop you. Don't let anybody tell you it has to be a certain way, you have to be like this or like that. Your life can be anything you want. You can do whatever you want to do, however you want to do it.
ANDY. Yeah, but…
KERNER. But nothing. That is your right. How dare anyone take that away from you. How dare anyone tell you what you feel is wrong. Shame on them, for anyone to interfere with something so fundamental, so precious. Pay no attention to it. I don't care where it's coming from. Do you understand?
ANDY. Yes.

KERNER. Hold on to that. Listen to your heart. Your dick'll be calling you, too, and that's fine…You know how to be careful? I mean really know.

ANDY. I'll study up.

KERNER. This is serious business.

ANDY. Yes. I know, I do.

KERNER. You'll have your experiences and that's great. But remember your heart. That's the name of the game.

ANDY. I will. I understand, I really do.

KERNER. Okay. Now forget about it because you don't have time.

ANDY. *(suddenly panicked)* What? Oh, God.

KERNER. Take it easy. All I'm saying is, don't let this stuff take over your life. Because it will if you let it. I have seen people destroyed – bright, talented people. I've seen them devote their whole lives to overcoming their so-called problem. By the time they've dealt with it, they're finished. All that energy that could have produced God-knows-what is wasted. Sucked out of them by society, their family, their own bullshit. How old are you now?

ANDY. Twenty.

KERNER. Still twenty?

ANDY. I guess it's a long year.

KERNER. You're in great shape. God, I'm so proud of you. I can't wait to see what happens.

ANDY. Me neither.

KERNER. Come here.

(KERNER pulls ANDY into an embrace.)

ANDY. Thank you.

KERNER. No. Thank you.

(They separate. KERNER looks at ANDY.)

I love you, Andy.

(It's uncertain where the moment will lead. Finally, KERNER leans in and kisses ANDY on the forehead, and then pushes him away.)

KERNER. Now go. Go find…what was it?

ANDY. Randy.

KERNER. Randy and Andy.

ANDY. I said it was stupid.

KERNER. You go find Randy and tell him you love him.

ANDY. I will. Thank you so much.

KERNER. Go.

(**ANDY** *hesitates.*)

ANDY. What do I do about my parents?

KERNER. What do you mean?

ANDY. Should I tell them? Maybe I should wait. I'll wait. Should I?

KERNER. Tell them or don't tell them. Either one, that's your decision. But don't spend another minute stewing over it. It's a waste of your energy and time.

ANDY. Which I don't have to spare.

KERNER. No one does.

ANDY. I'll tell them.

KERNER. And if they can't handle it, that's their problem. Not yours.

ANDY. Right.

KERNER. If you want me to be there, just let me know.

ANDY. Really? Wow…

KERNER. What?

ANDY. I was just trying to picture that.

(*Lights change as* **ANDY** *opens the door to reveal* **JOANNE** *and* **PETER**, *standing there with big smiles on their faces.*)

ANDY. Mom. Dad. I think you know Martin Kerner, the celebrated writer and director. We're here to tell you, I'm a homosexual.

KERNER. That's right, he is.

PETER. Well. This is a surprise.

JOANNE. One would have expected us to be upset, but somehow hearing this from the winner of six Tony Awards makes it happy news.

PETER. Son, if it's all right with Martin Kerner, it's all right with us.

(**ANDY** *closes the door on* **PETER** *and* **JOANNE**. *Lights change back to reality.*)

KERNER. I see what you mean.

ANDY. That doesn't mean I don't appreciate the offer.

KERNER. Well, I'm here if you need me.

ANDY. It should go okay, don't you think?

KERNER. I hope so.

ANDY. They must know on some level.

KERNER. That would be my guess.

ANDY. When did you know? When you saw me in a dress?

KERNER. No.

ANDY. No?

KERNER. When I read your letter.

ANDY. But…that was before I did.

KERNER. Not on some level.

ANDY. How could you tell?

KERNER. You did a lot of plays. And then there was the giveaway. You knew to find me. Good luck.

Scene Two

(JOANNE *addresses the audience.*)

JOANNE. He told us. I threw up. Believe me, I was just as surprised as you are. I was sick, not about Andy. About the way I felt. So...provincial. Peter, on the other hand, was wonderful, which was infuriating.

(**PETER** *enters.*)

PETER. Will you stop beating yourself up? We got over it, didn't we?

JOANNE. Yes, we did.

PETER. We took, what's-his-name –

JOANNE. Randy.

PETER. – Randy out to dinner, didn't we?

JOANNE. Yes, we did.

PETER. And let's face it, the idea of him bringing home a girl didn't thrill you either.

JOANNE. Not really, no.

PETER. We got over it. That's all there is to say about it.

JOANNE. *(to audience)* We got over it. Eventually.

(**ANDY** *enters.* **JOANNE** *and* **PETER** *stare at him.*)

ANDY. What?

JOANNE. Talk to us.

PETER. We miss you.

ANDY. Here I am.

JOANNE. We can't keep dancing around each other this way. Let's talk. All right? Okay? We'll talk about how you're feeling.

ANDY. I'm tired of talking. I'm tired of you interviewing me like I'm a Foreign Exchange Student and you're pretending to find my culture fascinating.

JOANNE. We're trying to understand...

ANDY. Well, stop. I told you the truth because I love you. But if you can't handle it, that's your problem, not mine. I don't have the energy or time to help you through it. I have to worry about my own development.

PETER. Who is giving you this stuff?

JOANNE. You know who. You talk to him about everything, don't you?

ANDY. He's been helping me. He's proud of me.

JOANNE. It's not his place to be proud of you.

ANDY. Fine.

JOANNE. What do you talk about? Sex? Is that it?

PETER. *(This gives him the willies.)* All right, let's not. This is embarrassing.

ANDY. Yes it is. What is the problem?

JOANNE. I don't like it. It isn't normal.

ANDY. Neither am I.

JOANNE. What is he getting from this?

ANDY. Dad was the one who told me to write to him.

JOANNE. I haven't forgotten that.

PETER. Uh-oh.

JOANNE. I don't think you should see him anymore.

ANDY. Are you serious? Dad?

PETER. Let's talk about this.

JOANNE. I'm not sure it's healthy.

ANDY. He invited me to sit in on some rehearsals. I'm going.

JOANNE. I don't think it's a good idea.

PETER. Joanne…

ANDY. This man is helping me have the life I always dreamed about. He thinks I've got the stuff, even if you don't. Fine. If you don't approve, I'm sure I can stay with Marty when I come to town from now on.

PETER. Stop that nonsense. This is where you belong.

ANDY. I used to think so. *(looks at* **JOANNE***, softens)* I know it's still really weird. It is for me, too. But it's not like I ran off and joined the Moonies. I'm still your son. It's not like I'm keeping stuff from you.

(The phone rings.)

I got it! It's for me, don't pick up, I got it!

(He runs offstage.)

PETER. What are you doing?
JOANNE. I don't like being shut out.
PETER. If he's going to be this way…
JOANNE. I can't do what you do.
PETER. Let go?
JOANNE. Give up.

Scene Three

*(**KERNER**'s office. **BRADLEY**'s at work, nervous. **JOANNE** enters.)*

JOANNE. Hello again.

BRADLEY. He can't see you.

JOANNE. So he's here.

BRADLEY. He's dealing with a problem. *Mad as Hell.*

JOANNE. What about?

BRADLEY. That's the name of the show. And that is the problem.

JOANNE. This won't take long.

BRADLEY. I let you up because I didn't want the doorman to throw you out. I didn't want you to be embarrassed.

JOANNE. How thoughtful.

BRADLEY. And because this gives me a chance to apologize. I remember I was rude to you that time you came here. I've always felt bad about it. I have my own mother issues and I shouldn't take them out on you. My mother would never have let me come here, let alone give me a lift.

JOANNE. Your mother sounds smart.

BRADLEY. I don't think so. She was never…a help. Anyway, I wanted to tell you that. I'm sorry.

JOANNE. Thank you.

BRADLEY. Now you have to leave.

JOANNE. I won't.

BRADLEY. Excuse me?

JOANNE. I came all this way. I'll wait.

BRADLEY. Mrs. Lipman, you're going to get me in a lot of trouble.

JOANNE. Well, that's too damn bad.

BRADLEY. I shouldn't have let you up.

JOANNE. Is that your job? To keep the mothers out? So the great man can amuse himself without interference?

BRADLEY. What are you talking about?

JOANNE. You think I don't know what's going on?

BRADLEY. I'm calling the doorman.

(BRADLEY picks up the building phone.)

JOANNE. What is he afraid of? That I might call the papers?

BRADLEY. *(into phone)* Walter? We've got a problem. This woman won't leave.

JOANNE. You'll have to drag me kicking and screaming, I swear to God! I'll tell the world what he's doing with my son!

(KERNER enters.)

KERNER. Is this because I didn't cast you?

BRADLEY. I told her you were busy...

KERNER. That's all right.

BRADLEY. *(into phone)* Never mind, Walter.

KERNER. Answer me. Is this because I didn't notice you in your purple leotard? Because you can't be here for this nonsense. It's beneath you.

JOANNE. My son wrote you a letter at sixteen. You waited two years to answer him. Why?

KERNER. A sixteen year-old boy living at home on Long Island? He wasn't ready for me to help him.

JOANNE. So you waited until he was eighteen. The legal age.

KERNER. What do you think you're doing?

JOANNE. I'm trying to pin down what's happening here.

KERNER. Well, don't! This is what I had to guard him against, this kind of...filth. You'd like it to be true. Then you could cry bloody murder and pull him away, keep him tied to your apron strings. But it's not that simple. This is far too nebulous, far too complex for you to condone or understand.

JOANNE. So, there's nothing...sexual, going on.

KERNER. It really is none of your business. But no. There doesn't happen to be anything sexual going on.

JOANNE. But there could have been.

KERNER. I don't like being accused!

(*Beat.* **JOANNE** *sits.*)

JOANNE. This is no good. I don't play the shocked, indignant mother very well, do I? You were right. That's not why I came.

KERNER. No?

JOANNE. When Andy was a little boy, Peter designed a theater for him in the basement where he'd put on plays and torture the neighbor children. He'd work so hard – cutting up my plaid skirt for a one-man *Brigadoon*... And afterwards, he would ask me into his bedroom, to huddle and tell him what I thought. You see, I was a professional, I'd been in summer stock, he'd seen the pictures. So, I'd give him my "notes." "Maybe it would have been better like this," or "Be careful to enunciate..." He was, I don't know, eight? Nine? And he'd listen so carefully. Peter would look in and call us Comden and Green. It was a happy time.

KERNER. Yes.

JOANNE. I want it back. I thought maybe you could help.

KERNER. Me? How?

JOANNE. Teach me. I see what you're giving him. The confidence, the appetite. I need that. Let me be part of it. Please.

KERNER. I'm sorry.

JOANNE. Why not? Why won't you take me on? Is it because I'm too old? Because I'm a woman?

KERNER. That has nothing to do with it.

JOANNE. Well, then, what is it? What is this world of talented gay men, passing on their secrets? I've seen it before, this closed society. Why won't you let me in?

KERNER. Because I can't! I don't have that much to give. I wish I did.

JOANNE. I don't understand.

KERNER. I don't have some endless supply of wisdom. I have…anecdotes. Tales from my experience, peppered with famous names. I have some common sense, no more than you do. But, it just so happens, the fact of who I am and what I represent puts me in a unique position. Andy came to me, and so have others, because I can give him what you can't. Permission. Permission to become himself, as fully as possible.

JOANNE. I want to give him that.

KERNER. But he can't receive it from you.

JOANNE. I'm just the mother.

KERNER. I'm afraid so. You know how it is. You're a teacher yourself.

JOANNE. With a boring old curriculum.

KERNER. I'm sure you find ways around that. To inspire.

JOANNE. I try.

KERNER. Me too.

JOANNE. Well, then. I suppose I should thank you. For taking the time.

KERNER. No need. That's not what I do it for.

JOANNE. What do you do it for?

KERNER. What?

JOANNE. Why do you take the time? Why do you make the phone calls, have the lunches? Andy gets the thrill of meeting his hero. He gets confidence, permission to be himself, all of it. What do you get?

KERNER. I get plenty. I get to look across the table at a beautiful, intelligent young face that sees nothing but the best of me, who knows nothing of my personal failures. I get to see the children I never had. I get to feel like I've accomplished something real, something that might last beyond my hectic little life. I get all that.

JOANNE. Not a bad deal.

KERNER. Not bad at all. Both sides walk away changed.

JOANNE. It's a kind of love, isn't it?

KERNER. It's quite a buzz, that's for sure. Is it sexual? You bet. Does that make it inappropriate? Not at all. I know, because I was on the other side of it once. I would be nothing today if someone important, someone I looked up to, hadn't taken me aside and said, "You've got the stuff, kid. Let me tell you what I know." Now it's my responsibility to do the same. This is how the culture is passed down, in Chinese restaurants and theater lobbies, at stage doors and rehearsal halls. So, I take the time. I sit with your sweet son and talk, and something important is kept alive. Be patient. He'll come to you when he's ready. And he'll have so many new things to tell you. Comden and Green will be back in business.

(*JOANNE is moved.* **KERNER** *breaks the mood.*)

KERNER. Bradley, you haven't had a line in eight pages.

BRADLEY. You were doing fine without me.

KERNER. Will you show Mrs. Lipman…?

JOANNE. Joanne. Please.

KERNER. Will you show Joanne out? I really must get back to work.

BRADLEY. Of course.

JOANNE. Mr. Kerner? I'm not sorry I came.

KERNER. Neither am I.

(**KERNER** *exits.*)

BRADLEY. He's a complicated man.

JOANNE. Yes, he is.

BRADLEY. He has a tendency to offer life-changing direction to people he doesn't know.

JOANNE. I've noticed.

BRADLEY. It was very brave of you to come here and talk to him that way. He appreciated that.

JOANNE. Well, I'm sure any parent would do the same.

BRADLEY. Are you kidding? Your son is very lucky.

JOANNE. You be sure to tell him that when he hears about this.

Scene Four

(ANDY berates his mother over the phone from his dorm room. PETER listens on another extension.)

ANDY. What were you imagining?! I go over it and over it in my mind trying to figure out what possessed you to go there. Menopause? Diet pills? Some sick desire to see your son die of sheer embarrassment?

PETER. Your mother doesn't take diet pills.

JOANNE. I wanted to talk to him.

ANDY. Dad?

PETER. I'm staying out of this.

ANDY. "A secret society of gay men?" How could you say that?

PETER. *(to JOANNE)* You said that? That doesn't sound good.

JOANNE. I thought you're staying out of this.

ANDY. Do you feel that threatened? Are you really afraid he'll take away your power over me? You're my mother. You can push my buttons and make me feel terrible any time you want for the rest of my life. Isn't that enough?

JOANNE. Well, it's a start.

(ANDY softens.)

ANDY. You're really something.

JOANNE. I'm sorry.

ANDY. Whatever. It's okay. I just get freaked out when my worlds collide.

JOANNE. It wasn't so bad. We had a nice conversation.

ANDY. I know. You made a good impression.

PETER. *(perking up, to JOANNE)* You hear that?

(to ANDY)

What did he say? What did he say about your mother?

ANDY. Dad...

PETER. What? I want to hear what he said exactly.

ANDY. You're both ridiculous.

PETER. Nice talk. Very nice.

ANDY. I have to go.

JOANNE. All right. We love you. Go study.

ANDY. Yeah. Oh, and, um, Mom? I finished the first draft of this play thing I'm writing. I was wondering, you always have a good sense, would you read it?

(Beat. **JOANNE** *is pleased.)*

JOANNE. Of course. Send it.

ANDY. I'm giving it to Kerner, but I'd like to get your notes first. All the people here are too artsy-fartsy.

JOANNE. I'll read it.

PETER. What about me? Am I too artsy-fartsy?

ANDY. You can read it, too. I gotta go. Bye.

(Lights out on **ANDY.** **PETER** *grins at* **JOANNE**, *who is thrilled but embarrassed.)*

JOANNE. I have papers to grade.

(She exits as **PETER** *laughs at her.)*

Scene Five

*(**KERNER** gives a rehearsal speech to the cast and crew of* Mad As Hell. **BRADLEY** *enters and organizes the tech table.* **ANDY** *takes a seat in separate area.)*

KERNER. All right, we're entering the home-stretch now.

ANDY. *(to audience)* I went to a rehearsal for *Mad As Hell*.

KERNER. I had an overly enthusiastic dentist who made me chew these little pink tablets that left colored marks anywhere I hadn't brushed properly. Well, that's the purpose of this run-through. We're going to find out where we haven't brushed.

*(**KERNER** sits down next to **BRADLEY**.)*

ANDY. *(to audience)* I expected to see admiration, even love on the faces of the cast and crew. I didn't. Oh, well, tensions are always high before the first preview.

*(**BRADLEY** whispers to **KERNER** who turns and sees **ANDY**. **ANDY** waves. **KERNER** nods and turns back toward the rehearsal (downstage). We hear sounds of the show under what follows.)*

(to audience) It opened well, Kerner shows always did. I waited for him to fix something on the spot, reinvent a moment, change a line. But it never happened. Instead, Kerner read the paper.

*(**KERNER** takes out a copy of the* New York Times *and begins to read.* **BRADLEY** *continues to watch and take notes.)*

(to audience) He never looked up. Bradley had to give him a nudge at the end of Act One.

*(**BRADLEY** nudges **KERNER** who looks up at the rehearsal.)*

(to audience) He went back to the paper for Act Two. Except for when he fell asleep.

*(**KERNER** sleeps. **BRADLEY** takes more notes.)*

(to audience) I gotta admit, I didn't blame him.

(Lights up on **PETER** *and* **JOANNE** *playing the roles of* **DIANA** *(Faye Dunaway) and* **MAX** *(William Holden). She puts on earrings and smokes. He drinks and watches her. Music under.)*

JOANNE (AS DIANA). I spoke to Sybil the Soothsayer. She predicts a thirty share for the news hour…provided Howard goes crazy again, which he damn well better. Did you see the overnights? The ratings are fantastic!

PETER (AS MAX). Jesus H. Christ, Diana. Ratings, points and shares. Can you think of nothing else?

JOANNE (AS DIANA). Oh, Max, don't get high and mighty with me. I like screwing a father figure, not listening to one.

(He slaps her. Beat. Then they kiss wildly and he grabs her ass.)

I need you, Max.

PETER (AS MAX). I'll tell you what you need.

(Musical intro to a song. **PETER** *opens his mouth to sing and the lights on them go out.)*

ANDY. *(to audience)* I couldn't wait for it to end.

(The rehearsal ends. Lights change.)

KERNER. You get everything down?

BRADLEY. I think so.

KERNER. Type them up. I need them for dinner with the others.

BRADLEY. You want to let everybody go?

KERNER. It's too late now.

BRADLEY. I meant tonight.

KERNER. Oh.

(to the company) All right, thank you. I think we learned a lot. You can all get out of here.

(seeing **ANDY***)*

Hey, kid.

BRADLEY. Hi, Andy. Glad you made it.

ANDY. Thank you so much for letting me come.

(**KERNER** *gives him a social kiss on the cheek.*)

KERNER. You're brightening my day, believe me. You look terrific. How's Randy?

ANDY. He's great.

KERNER. I could use a Randy about now. You two are still all over each other I bet.

ANDY. Sort of...

KERNER. Look, you're blushing. That's cute. God, I'd love to see you two together. You should bring him opening night.

ANDY. He'd love that.

KERNER. If we ever make it.

ANDY. The opening number is great.

KERNER. You think so?

ANDY. And I was fascinated by how you work.

KERNER. How do you mean?

ANDY. You take such a...laissez-faire approach...at least, that's how it looks on the surface.

KERNER. I've gotten to the point on this one where I don't have to watch anymore. I just know. It's in the air. You pick it up whether you want to or not. You'll see.

ANDY. I hope so. I'll have to start soon, though. I graduate in June.

KERNER. Oh, Jesus. You're kidding. Already?

ANDY. I'll be twenty-two in three weeks.

KERNER. Unbelievable.

ANDY. The clock is ticking. And I really want to get something going before graduation so I don't end up answering phones in my Dad's office.

KERNER. I have a feeling you'll make out okay.

ANDY. Yeah, you've said that before.

KERNER. Bradley, how am I doing on time?

BRADLEY. Okay. But if you want to return these calls...

KERNER. Oh, right.

ANDY. Have you had a chance to read my play?

KERNER. What? Didn't I tell you? Oh, Andy. Yes, I did.

ANDY. Oh, great, you read it, you did.

KERNER. I think it's very funny, full of heart. A little too clever in places but such a freshness to it. I was tickled by it.

ANDY. Wow. That makes me so…Look, I know you're crazed, but I'd love to talk about it in detail with you. To see where I should go from here.

KERNER. I don't want to do that.

ANDY. What? Why?

KERNER. You're on a journey with that script. I'll wait and see what the next draft looks like.

ANDY. Oh. I wasn't…okay. I was just thinking, maybe we could show it to that agent, Florence Green.

KERNER. Florence wouldn't get it, believe me. Besides, she doesn't do shit for her clients these days.

ANDY. Okay. Well, I'll send it to you when I have something.

KERNER. I can't wait. I've got to get ready for dinner with the producers. Bradley, find some time for me to talk to Andy. I want to hear his notes.

BRADLEY. Sure thing.

(**KERNER** *gathers his things to leave.*)

ANDY. Marty, I hate to bring it up, but you said something about calling people at the regionals about me.

KERNER. The regionals? No, you don't want to get stuck at a regional, writing program notes for *Can't Take it With You*. That's not for you.

ANDY. But you said…

KERNER. The regionals do crap. We'll come up with something else.

(**KERNER** *puts on his jacket and starts to exit.*)

ANDY. Oh. Okay. Because June is just around the corner.

KERNER. I'll think about it.

ANDY. Thank you. When do you think you might have some idea…?

(**ANDY**'s gone too far. **KERNER** turns on him.)

KERNER. All right, Andy, that's enough! For Christ's sake, you see I'm busy. I said I'd think about it. You're very pushy, you know that? You have to learn to control that impulse. Otherwise nobody will ever work with you.

ANDY. I'm sorry.

KERNER. This always happens. You become insatiable. Needy little monsters. Nothing's ever enough.

ANDY. I'm sorry. Marty, please…

KERNER. I've got to go! Bradley, you'll bring me those notes.

(to **ANDY**) Don't push.

(**KERNER** exits.)

ANDY. He promised me. He did. I'm not crazy.

BRADLEY. This is not a referral agency. The sooner you understand that, the better off you'll be.

ANDY. So all that stuff about working together…

BRADLEY. He talks big, maybe without thinking things through. He's careless. Is that a crime? Sometimes things do work out.

ANDY. I feel so stupid.

BRADLEY. Don't. He may surprise you.

ANDY. I think I just blew it.

BRADLEY. Nah. Today was just a bad day. The show's in trouble, we all know it. And Timothy fell off the wagon last week. He had been doing really well, but there was a party, open bar, and the next thing we knew…

ANDY. Wait. Who's Timothy?

BRADLEY. (surprised **ANDY** doesn't know) Timothy is Marty's lover.

ANDY. Oh. God. I didn't know he was seeing someone.

BRADLEY. He is. For about thirty years.

ANDY. Why didn't he tell me?

BRADLEY. You don't get all of him. No one does. I think he's closer to you than most. Still, he's always careful. This is very difficult for him.

ANDY. For him?

BRADLEY. Everyone wants something from him. He pays a price for being approachable. Some real crazies and hangers-on accumulate like flies. You've always been good at knowing how far to go with him. Timing is very important. Don't lose that.

ANDY. Thanks for the tip.

BRADLEY. No problem.

ANDY. I've always wondered, how did you and Marty get together?

BRADLEY. Oh. I wrote him a letter.

(Beat.)

ANDY. You mean…?

BRADLEY. Yeah.

ANDY. What happened?

BRADLEY. He took me to lunch. We talked about the theater, my future…I was going to be the next Mike Nichols. Then one day, he told me he had come to a decision about me. He said I would make a great assistant. I might be able to have the big career if I fought for it, if I wanted it badly enough. But I'd also make a great assistant.

ANDY. What a terrible thing to say.

BRADLEY. That's what I thought. I decided, I'll show him. I'll go out there and… well, you know the rest. I didn't have the confidence, the support. I didn't have the need. And he was right. I make a great assistant.

ANDY. Well, hey, if you're okay with that…

BRADLEY. Don't patronize me.

ANDY. I'm sorry.

BRADLEY. I'm lucky. I don't need to see my name in the paper to prove I exist. I don't walk around feeling like I'm less than I'm supposed to be. I live and work in the world I love without the curse.

ANDY. You are lucky.

BRADLEY. Things worked out. Try to understand. The fact that he's not taking you under his wing may not be so bad in the long run. Take care of yourself, Andy. Do it yourself.

ANDY. Thank you.

BRADLEY. Don't mention it.

(holds up his pad)

I better go. He needs me.

*(***BRADLEY** *exits.)*

Scene Six

(The phone rings. Lights up on **ANDY** *in his college dorm room.* **KERNER** *appears at home, wearing a tuxedo, drunk. It's very late.)*

ANDY. Hello?

KERNER. Andy? It's Marty.

ANDY. Oh…Hi.

KERNER. I got your telegram. That was very sweet. Very sweet.

ANDY. My pleasure. It felt so Broadway, sending a telegram on opening night. So, how did it go?

KERNER. We're dead. I'm dead.

ANDY. Oh, come on, that's not true.

KERNER. Did you read that schmuck in the *Times? (reading from the newspaper)* "The sad spectacle of an aging artist trying to pass as a cool young hipster, like Ronald Reagan in Jordache Jeans."

ANDY. How many times have you told me? Critics don't matter…

KERNER. It's the British. That's what it is. The fucking British.

ANDY. The British?

KERNER. People don't know quality anymore. They want light shows and giant junk-heaps.

ANDY. You're so right.

KERNER. The show isn't perfect, I know that. But it was flawed at its inception, long before they called me. I came on as a favor. You should never do anything in your career because of personal relationships. Loyalty and affection have no place in this business, you hear me, Andy?

ANDY. Yeah. I hear you.

KERNER. So now I'm fucked, I'm a has-been. They think it's my fault, as if I had full control over what's up there. An artist has power over x-percent of his work. You try to raise x as high as you can, but that's it. And as hard as you try, it's never enough. Sometimes you're fucked no matter what. Remember that.

ANDY. I will.

KERNER. But does anyone out there understand that? No. They're too busy licking their chops, ready to shoot you down, to nail you to the wall. You can't stay on top for long because they don't like that.

ANDY. Maybe it's partly generational, you know…

KERNER. What the fuck is that? You're saying I'm too old?

ANDY. No, I just meant…

KERNER. What? "You meant." You think I can't keep up with the new guys? I'm over-the-hill? Let me tell you something, they're still behind what I was doing twenty years ago! Way behind!

ANDY. Marty, please. I think you're the greatest. But you just said, people don't know quality anymore.

KERNER. Exactly.

ANDY. Look at all the incredible things you've accomplished. Nobody can take that away from you.

KERNER. Time takes care of that. You'll see. You think you have some hits and you're made for life. But you still have to get up every morning and ask, "What the fuck am I going to do today?" It never ends. It's never enough.

ANDY. I guess not.

KERNER. I have to reinvent myself, do something new.

ANDY. Maybe I can help.

KERNER. Yeah. I'd like that. Ah, listen to me ranting like a lunatic, I'm…How are you doing, kid?

ANDY. Okay, I guess. It looks like I'll be living at home for a while, after graduation. I'll send out resumes while I work in my dad's office. Save some money till Randy finishes.

KERNER. You and Randy are still together. That's beautiful.

ANDY. Yeah. And some friends and I are going to start a group to put up stuff. I want to be more experimental. I'm working on something, *The Ballad of Archie*, I'd love you to see it.

KERNER. So is Randy there now?

ANDY. No, he's pulling an all-nighter, writing a paper.

KERNER. Those were the days. Hey, tell me, does Randy have a pretty dick?

ANDY. *(flustered)* I don't...I guess, yeah.

KERNER. What? I embarrass you? You think I'm a dirty old man?

ANDY. No.

KERNER. I thought we were friends.

ANDY. We are. I just, no one's ever...

KERNER. Ah, fuck, fuck, fuck! The fuckin' British...

(**KERNER** *trails off. Pause.*)

ANDY. Marty? Are you okay?

KERNER. Yeah. I'm peachy. I wish I could see your face.

ANDY. Maybe when I come to New York...

KERNER. Can't. I'm going away. I need to get away from all this shit. The house in Rome...A year or two, something...

ANDY. Oh, God. Rome.

KERNER. They have phones now. I won't forget you.

ANDY. I'll miss you.

KERNER. I'll miss you, too, kid. You give me such a kick...

(**KERNER** *suddenly regrets the call.*)

KERNER. *(to himself)* Jesus, what was I thinking? *(to* **ANDY**, *friendly)* It's late. Thanks for the telegram.

ANDY. Have a good trip.

KERNER. Keep up the good work.

(*as he hangs up*)

I have to figure out what to do now.

Scene Seven

(The Ballad of Archie. **PETER** *appears as an actor playing "Father." He wears an ugly, mismatched outfit and speaks in a broad, exaggerated manner.)*

PETER AS FATHER. Ar-chie?! Ar-chie?! It's bonding time. Ar-chie?! What do you say we throw a ball around?

*(***ANDY** *appears as "Son." He wears a Silence=Death T-shirt.)*

ANDY AS SON. I can't throw a ball. I could never throw a ball. What are you imagining?

PETER AS FATHER. So, when are we going to meet your girlfriend?

ANDY AS SON. There is no girlfriend. I like guys. I like them naked.

PETER AS FATHER. Okay, just one game. One-on-one.

ANDY AS SON. I like them in the shower. I like them on top of me.

PETER AS FATHER. You bring your girlfriend over. Your mother'll make us something special.

*(***JOANNE** *enters as "Mother." She wears a purple tutu and dances throughout the scene.)*

JOANNE AS MOTHER. Get your own damn "something special." I was born to dance!

PETER AS FATHER. Your mother is a wonderful dancer, son.

JOANNE AS MOTHER. Out of my way!

ANDY AS SON. Then what is she doing here?

JOANNE AS MOTHER. Suffering! Suffering for you! Every minute of my stinking life!

PETER AS FATHER. What about tether-ball? I could tie one onto a tree.

ANDY AS SON. What am I doing here? I can't breathe!

JOANNE AS MOTHER. Where are you going?

ANDY AS SON. The nearest truck stop. I need dick!

JOANNE AS MOTHER. Oh! I'm gonna be sick! Aaaaaah!

(She dances offstage to throw up, which we hear her do, noisily.)

PETER AS FATHER. Doesn't mean she doesn't love you, son.

ANDY AS SON. Of course not. Why would I think that?

*(He turns and skips off. **PETER** takes center stage and acts up a storm.)*

PETER AS FATHER. I just wanted to play some ball. Is that so much to ask? Is that so goddam much? Is that so goddam much?

*(Lights out. The show is over. Scattered applause. Lights up on **JOANNE** and **PETER** waiting after the performance, fiddling with their programs, nonplussed. **ANDY** comes out to greet them. He seems changed. Darker.)*

ANDY. Hey. Pretty "out there," huh?

PETER. That's one way of putting it.

ANDY. I figured it wasn't your cup of tea. But I'm really going after it, getting in touch with my anger.

JOANNE. Very provocative.

*(**ANDY** is hurt by the brush-off.)*

PETER. All right, let's go. I want to see if the car's still there. What's the story? Are you coming with us?

ANDY. No. I'm going out with some friends. People who aren't afraid to talk about what they saw.

JOANNE. Oh, Andy, come on.

PETER. We're just stupid suburbanites.

JOANNE. Stupid, straight suburbanites.

PETER. You don't care what we think.

ANDY. Of course I do. You're my parents. I care a lot.

PETER. Okay. We didn't like it. No big deal. You win some you lose some. You were right. It's not our cup of tea.

ANDY. Mom?

JOANNE. The shows are getting so ugly.

ANDY. "Ugly."

JOANNE. Compared to what you used to do. Peter, let's go, I'm tired.

ANDY. I can't believe this. Do you know how hurtful you're being?

PETER. Hey, you asked us...

ANDY. How can you do this to me?

JOANNE. What have we done to you? We're the ones who had to sit through this garbage.

PETER. All right, that's a bit strong.

JOANNE. He attacks and humiliates us and then wants us to tell him how wonderful he is. Well, I can't do it anymore.

PETER. See that, Andy? The play made your mother upset. You got a strong reaction. Isn't that what you were looking for?

ANDY. Yes, as a matter of fact.

JOANNE. Well, then congratulations. Maybe next time I'll throw up again. Then you can retire in triumph.

ANDY. Oh, you'd like that, wouldn't you? You'd like me to quit like you did.

JOANNE. What did you say?

ANDY. I know what this is. You're just jealous because I'm living the life of an artist. I'm really doing it, the way you wanted to but couldn't.

JOANNE. At least when I danced, I got paid for it.

ANDY. You would measure success that way.

JOANNE. Seems like a good place to start.

PETER. All right, stop it, both of you. Look Andy, your mother's mad, we both are. You hurt our feelings. This used to be fun for us, coming to your shows.

ANDY. Oh, so everything you've ever done has been for what you get out of it. Not what I need.

PETER. That's not fair.

JOANNE. We don't give you what you need? All right. What you need now is to be treated like an adult. Like someone who can face the truth.

ANDY. *(to himself)* Capital 'T.'

JOANNE. You think you're all courageous, "getting in touch with your anger." Well, there's only one problem. You have nothing to be angry about. You write about us, make fun of us? You don't know us. You don't even know yourself. You're just a self-centered boy who's furious because the world isn't rolling out the red carpet anymore. Either find something real to be angry about or shut up!

(Pause. Everyone feels terrible.)

PETER. Obviously, if you're trying to please us, you're going about it the wrong way. And you know something, that's probably not the right motivation anyway.

JOANNE. You should listen to your father. He's been behind you all along. He never turned away.

ANDY. I know.

JOANNE. He's not jealous of you like I am. It's true. I am.

ANDY. You shouldn't be.

*(**ANDY** turns to leave.)*

PETER. Hey, where you going?

ANDY. I let everybody down.

*(**ANDY** walks off.)*

PETER. You don't think we were a little tough on him?

JOANNE. Whatever we do is wrong.

Scene Eight

(In the dark we hear another radio news program, this time circa 1988. Something about Michael Dukakis.)

(Lights up again on the family having breakfast. **ANDY** *has changed further. He's listless, sullen.* **PETER** *still has his* Times.*)*

JOANNE. What time will you be home tonight?

ANDY. I don't know.

JOANNE. Are you coming home?

ANDY. I don't know. Pierre and I are doing some stuff for the magazine. We're going to a rally.

JOANNE. I don't like that Pierre.

ANDY. Quel suprise.

PETER. Your mother's right. Your friend Pierre's an obnoxious kid.

ANDY. He's almost thirty.

PETER. That makes it worse.

JOANNE. *(trying to be upbeat)* So you're working on the magazine. Anything else happening?

ANDY. Nothing's happening. Nothing ever happens.

PETER. What about your friends in California? Have you heard from any of them?

ANDY. I'm not interested!

JOANNE. I don't know why you think it's such a horrible thing, if that's where things are happening…

PETER. *(seeing an item in the paper)* Hey, here's something about your friend Kerner.

JOANNE. What's he doing?

PETER. *(reads a bit, then)* He's… oh…

*(***JOANNE*** takes the paper and reads aloud.)*

JOANNE. "Broadway writer and director Martin Kerner will mount an Off-Broadway production of Georg Büchner's Expressionist classic, *Woyzeck*. Kerner, who was last represented by *Mad as Hell*, the ill-fated musical based on the film *Network*…"

PETER. He'll never live that down.

JOANNE. "...will oversee the work of controversial young director, Bruce Radford..."

ANDY. Oh, no! No, no, no!

(to **JOANNE***)* Keep going.

JOANNE. "Radford, twenty-five...

ANDY. He's gotta be twenty-six at least!

JOANNE. "...first staged the play as an undergraduate at Harvard University. That production is remembered for being performed entirely in a dormitory swimming pool."

PETER. That bastard.

(Lights up on **KERNER***.)*

KERNER. "Bruce is a unique talent."

JOANNE. "...said Kerner, speaking from his New York office..."

ANDY. He's back?

KERNER. "We met some time ago and I've been watching his development. It's always a pleasure to help a gifted young artist reach his audience. I think of it as my responsibility to nurture..."

ANDY. Stop!

(Lights out on **KERNER***.)*

PETER. Did you know this guy, Radford?

ANDY. It doesn't matter.

JOANNE. Boy, he loves to play the magnanimous big-shot. You see what he's doing. He wants to do something weird so he won't look like the fossil he is.

PETER. Andy?

ANDY. That's show-biz.

*(***ANDY*** walks off.)*

PETER. Son-of-a-bitch.

JOANNE. We're the ones who encouraged him his whole life, told him he was the best at everything.

PETER. As opposed to what? Calling him an idiot? Oh, that's much healthier. I guess my parents knew what they were doing after all.

JOANNE. Don't twist this around. If his dreams fall to pieces, what will happen to him?

PETER. He'll be like the rest of us.

Scene Nine

*(A phone rings. **BRADLEY** answers and speaks to **ANDY**. All signs of the sweet, preppy kid from Act One have disappeared.)*

BRADLEY. Martin Kerner's office.

ANDY. Bradley, hi, it's Andy. Lipman.

BRADLEY. Oh, hi! How are you doing? How's the real world treating you?

ANDY. Not too well, I'm afraid. Things haven't worked out.

BRADLEY. I'm sorry to hear that.

ANDY. Yeah, well. It happens.

BRADLEY. Hang in there. We all have faith in you.

ANDY. I've heard. Look, Bradley, I need to see him. I know he's back. Can I see him?

BRADLEY. I don't know. Things are pretty crazy...

ANDY. Come on, please. You know how long it's been? I won't ask him for a job, if that's what you're worried about.

BRADLEY. Of course not...

ANDY. I have something I need to talk to him about. He owes me that much.

BRADLEY. It's just a scheduling thing...

ANDY. All right, fine, whatever.

BRADLEY. No, wait. He's got a production meeting at the Minetta Lane tomorrow that should end early. I'll tell him to wait for you. I won't let him cancel.

ANDY. Thank you.

BRADLEY. No problem. But can I just say one thing? Nobody owes anybody anything.

*(Lights out on **BRADLEY**. Lights up on the Minetta Lane. There's a table with **KERNER**'s things. **ANDY** walks to the center of the stage and looks around.)*

ANDY. Hello? Is anybody here?

*(**KERNER** appears at the back of the house.)*

KERNER. There he is. My God. What has happened to that boy who came to lunch? He's a man now. Standing alone on a bare stage. How does it feel?

ANDY. Empty.

KERNER. Then fill it.

(ANDY holds his arms out and stands a little taller, with more presence.)

There you go. Hey, kid.

(KERNER steps up onto the stage.)

ANDY. Hi, Marty. How are you?

KERNER. Me?

ANDY. Yeah, you. I never get to ask how you are. How's your life?

KERNER. I'm perfect. My life is fantastic. Thanks for asking.

ANDY. How's Timothy?

KERNER. He's fine. Doing well.

ANDY. I'm glad to hear it.

KERNER. This is different. You're talking to me like an old friend.

ANDY. I am an old friend.

KERNER. Yes, you are. It gives me such a kick.

ANDY. It's been a while.

KERNER. Well, I figured you needed some time without me looking over your shoulder. You don't need me coddling you, you get that elsewhere. How old are you now?

ANDY. Just turned twenty-four.

KERNER. Jesus. I hate to think what that makes me.

ANDY. You never change.

KERNER. Flattery will get you anywhere.

ANDY. That's what I'm hoping.

KERNER. So. What's up? Bradley tells me you're having a rough time.

ANDY. It's not how I pictured it, that's all.

KERNER. It never is. There are always obstacles. Every generation has its cross to bear. Whether it's war, Depression, a witch-hunt...

ANDY. A plague.

KERNER. Exactly. This could be good for you. Really feel what you're feeling. Take it all in and move ahead. Like we've always said.

ANDY. "Really face it."

KERNER. You got it.

ANDY. That's actually why I'm here.

KERNER. Oh?

ANDY. I was kind of jealous when I heard how you're helping Bruce Radford...

KERNER. A situation presented itself. I wanted to do something experimental, he had something ready to go... Who knows, at some point, when you're ready...

ANDY. Don't. Please. I realize things may not go so quickly for me.

KERNER. A lot of the greats were slow starters.

ANDY. I'm adjusting.

KERNER. Good.

ANDY. I've been writing for a magazine.

KERNER. Really? Which one?

ANDY. It's called *Open*.

KERNER. I'm not familiar with it.

ANDY. It's gay. It's a gay magazine. My friend Pierre is the editor and he asked me to contribute to the Arts section.

KERNER. Oh. I see.

ANDY. The magazine has done some excellent work.

KERNER. Well, if you're involved, I don't doubt it.

ANDY. Pierre and I had an idea.

KERNER. Yes?

ANDY. We thought I could interview you. Give you a forum to tell it like it is. The way you've done with me all these years.

KERNER. You mean…?

ANDY. It occurred to us that you've never officially come out in the press. I mean, you haven't, have you?

KERNER. I don't remember doing so.

ANDY. That's what we thought. Now, obviously we would never just "out" you against your will. But we think this would be a marvelous opportunity.

KERNER. For whom?

ANDY. Well, for the magazine, of course. But for you, too. And for all the gay kids out there who are growing up without role models. You can do for them what you did for me.

KERNER. And this is what you wanted to talk to me about. Why you called Bradley in such a state.

ANDY. Well… yes.

KERNER. Thank you for thinking of me. But I'm not interested.

*(**KERNER** gathers his things to leave.)*

ANDY. Why not?

KERNER. I'm not a politician, I'm an artist.

ANDY. Meaning?

KERNER. I don't care to "identify" myself as one thing or another. It's not how I wish to spend my time.

ANDY. But think about how useful it would be for you to be recognized.

KERNER. I am recognized. When I throw a party at the house on Fire Island, do you think I'm sending out mixed signals?

ANDY. Of course not.

KERNER. Why should I push a private part of myself on people who'll never understand it? If they could, they'd know already. Andy, I've given you my answer.

ANDY. Well, I'm sorry, but I don't accept that.

KERNER. That's too fucking bad.

*(**KERNER** steps off the stage and heads to the exit.)*

ANDY. All these years, I've listened to you rail against "camp." Anything you didn't like was "camp," the lowest of the low. Now it makes sense.

(KERNER stops and faces ANDY.)

KERNER. Oh, I'm self-hating, is that it?

ANDY. You never even mentioned Timothy to me. What are you ashamed of?

KERNER. Oh, Christ. I beg your pardon, but you're giving me a lecture I don't think I need. I am a gay man! There, I said it. But I will only say it on my terms.

ANDY. Which are?

(KERNER steps back onstage.)

KERNER. One-on-one. For people who can taste it, feel it, touch it. Anything else doesn't interest me.

ANDY. You could be a role model.

KERNER. I am a role model. Haven't I been effective with you?

ANDY. But think of the world.

KERNER. Fuck the world!

ANDY. "Fuck the world?" How can you say that? How can you turn your back on people who need you?

KERNER. You don't know what you're talking about. You don't know shit. You don't know how many beautiful boys I've seen put in the ground. You don't know the money I give.

ANDY. No, I don't. So, tell me. Tell everyone.

KERNER. I don't care to.

ANDY. Can't you understand what a difference it would make, to grow up in a world where everyone knew Martin Kerner was gay? Where even your mother couldn't miss it...

KERNER. Your mother doesn't miss much.

ANDY. Even she didn't talk about it.

KERNER. What is this obsession with your mother? You want to be an artist and you're still worrying about Mom? I've never heard of such a thing.

ANDY. Are you serious? What about Tennessee Williams?

KERNER. Please. You'll never be in his league.

(Beat. ANDY is stung, more than he wishes to show. KERNER regrets what he said.)

ANDY. I know. But I liked it better when everything was possible.

KERNER. *(softer, contrite)* Look, Andy, you upset me. It makes me mean. You came at me too strong. Maybe Randy finds it a turn on, but I don't.

ANDY. It's over with Randy. He dumped me.

KERNER. Andy, I'm sorry. What happened?

ANDY. He got everything he wanted. When I had nothing more to teach, he turned away.

(KERNER smiles at the irony.)

ANDY. You don't have to be so happy about it.

KERNER. I'm not. But now I know what all this is about.

ANDY. What?

KERNER. I can't protect you from heartbreak. I wouldn't if I could. You're hurt, you're angry, the career isn't happening, you're writing for the "queer press" for God's sake.

ANDY. That has nothing to do with it. This is important.

KERNER. This is politics. You're at that stage. You want to save the world, great. Just don't let it obliterate the rest.

ANDY. Shit. I knew you wouldn't do it. You never do anything.

(He starts to go. KERNER stops him.)

KERNER. Oh, so you came here to test me. To label me a hypocrite and walk out the hero. Well, I'm afraid it's not as grand as that, my not-so-young friend.

ANDY. I'm doing what's right.

KERNER. Bullshit. You're afraid you can't hack it, so you're taking it out on me. Well, if that's the way you want it, go ahead. But then I can't help you any more.

ANDY. Help me? How have you helped me? Tell me, please!

KERNER. I encouraged you...

ANDY. Yes, you encouraged me. You filled my head with promises of things I would never do. You prepared me for a glorious career in a world that no longer exists!

KERNER. I won't take responsibility for that.

ANDY. Why should you? No matter what, you come out a winner. If I succeed, it's your success – "Oh, that Martin Kerner, what an eye for talent." If I fail, it's all my fault. Well, I'm failing, Marty. Can you encourage me now? What's to become of me now?

KERNER. You're not Eliza Doolittle and I'm not your Henry Higgins. You're a smart Jewish boy from the suburbs. I thought you could be more than that. If I was wrong, I apologize.

ANDY. I want to be more than that! I want to make my mark! But you never tell me what I'm supposed to do!

KERNER. Of course not! Don't you understand? I'm not teaching you what to do. I'm trying to teach you how to be!

(with great feeling) I don't care what you do with your career. As long as you preserve what's in there.

*(He taps **ANDY**'s heart.)*

Your love. Your sense of humor, your point of view. You can work in a shoe store, I don't give a damn. What you carry around inside you, that's what I care about. And I'll do anything I can to keep that alive, to keep you from wrapping yourself in anger and cynicism. That's my part of the bargain. Always has been.

ANDY. *(filled with mixed emotions)* Well, I'm sorry, but I can't keep up my end of the bargain anymore. I can't worship you.

*(**KERNER** slaps **ANDY** across the face. Beat.)*

KERNER. Now look what you've done. Goodbye, Andy.

*(**KERNER** turns to leave. **ANDY** runs to **KERNER** and throws his arms around him.)*

ANDY. I'm sorry. Marty, I'm sorry. I didn't mean it. I've been so lucky to have you.

KERNER. *(pushing him away)* No. It's over.

*(**KERNER** steps off the stage and starts to exit. He stops and looks back at **ANDY**.)*

Don't worry. You're going to do just fine.

Scene Ten

(JOANNE addresses the audience.)

JOANNE. He didn't tell us what happened. He said he would when he was ready but he moved away before then. He was just going out to visit friends and before we knew it, he was only coming home for Thanksgiving. I don't know if Andy ever spoke to Kerner again. But Peter did.

(Lights upon PETER talking to ANDY on the phone in California. ANDY is in his office. He looks comfortable with himself at last, hip.)

PETER. Hey, you'll never guess who I ran into on the street.

ANDY. Who?

PETER. What's-his-name. Your old friend, Kerner.

ANDY. Oh, God. How'd he look?

PETER. The same. I told him about you.

ANDY. Dad, you didn't.

(The scene shifts to 45th street. KERNER walks by PETER who recognizes him. ANDY still listens on the phone.)

PETER. Mr. Kerner? Excuse me.

KERNER. Yes?

PETER. Peter Lipman. Andy's father.

KERNER. Oh, yes. How are you?

PETER. Fine. I should have figured I'd see you in the theater district. Are you working on a new show?

KERNER. Always.

PETER. I'm here for meetings about a hotel we're designing in Times Square. Don't worry, we won't tear down another theater.

KERNER. I doubt anyone would notice if you did.

PETER. You think?

KERNER. There's almost nothing left of the theater beyond its ability to make you feel guilty doing anything else.

ANDY. He said that?

PETER. I don't know if you've heard from Andy…

KERNER. No, I haven't.

PETER. He's doing great. He moved out to L.A., got a job writing for a TV show. And next season they're letting him direct. Can you imagine, for a twenty-six year-old kid?

KERNER. Well, that's how they operate out there.

PETER. I'm so proud of him, the way he did it on his own, without any help.

ANDY. You didn't say that!

PETER. *(to* **ANDY***)* Of course I did. He should know, the son-of-a-bitch. *(to* **KERNER***, charming again)* Listen, I'm sure Andy would love to hear from you. Do you want his address?

KERNER. Thank you, that won't be necessary. If you'll excuse me.

*(***KERNER*** exits.* **PETER** *returns to the phone call.)*

PETER. He acted like he couldn't get away fast enough.

ANDY. I wonder why.

PETER. You should write to him. Maybe you could give him a summer job.

*(***PETER*** exits.* **ANDY** *addresses the audience.)*

ANDY. I did write to him. After I read his autobiography: *Kerner: Confessions of a Flash in the Pan.*

(He picks up a copy.)

When it came out, I ran to the bookstore and checked the acknowledgements, searching for my name.

(He finds a page.)

"And finally, to Andrew Lipman, who helped me focus, my deepest thanks." It wasn't there.

(He puts the book down.)

ANDY. Not in the index either. I bought it anyway. It was a fun read. One of those books that feels brutally honest without actually being so. Details of his private life were there, but always in a way your mother could miss them. Well, not my mother…It was what I expected, except for one surprise. How much I missed him. I wrote him a letter.

*(Lights shift as **ANDY** speaks his letter.)*

"Dear Marty, Can you believe it's been ten years since I first wrote to you? A mediocre decade has come and gone. First, let me congratulate you on your book. It was such a pleasure to hear your voice again, telling my favorite stories.

*(Lights up on **BRADLEY** in **KERNER**'s office, opening **ANDY**'s letter.)*

"Second, let me apologize for my behavior the last time we met. I still believe what I said, but I shouldn't have been so rude. And I was wrong about one thing. I said you never helped me. You did.

*(**KERNER** enters. **BRADLEY** hands him the letter.)*

BRADLEY. It's from Andy Lipman.

*(**KERNER** reads.)*

ANDY. "I see it now, every day. Wherever I go, whatever I see, read, or think, is filtered through what I learned from you. Those lunches and late-night phone calls gave me the tools to look, and to make something of what I find.

*(**BRADLEY** exits, leaving **KERNER** alone with the letter.)*

"My life is very comfortable now, here in the wasteland. I'm overpaid in a job I don't respect, which I struggled to get and am afraid to lose. I wonder, will I ever do anything of value? Will anything ever happen with those plays I keep writing in the middle of the night? And then, just as I'm about to get really depressed, there will be a fight on set. Some network schmuck will want to change a moment somehow I know will make it worse. And I won't let him. I fight to make it better, to bring it just a bit closer to the truth, small "t." And at those moments, Marty, that's when I know what I got from you. That's when I remember the sweet kid in the khaki pants who really cared. Is it enough? No. You taught me, it's never enough. But it's something. Thank you for that. I hope we're still friends.

"Love, Andy."

(**KERNER** *looks at* **ANDY**. *The lights fade on* **KERNER**.)

I never heard from him.

(*A phone rings.* **ANDY** *answers. Lights up on* **JOANNE** *at home.*)

ANDY. Yeah?

JOANNE. Hi, it's me. What's doing?

ANDY. I'm busy, Ma, what's up?

JOANNE. They're putting in metal detectors at the school. Can you believe it?

ANDY. Amazing.

JOANNE. I think it's time for me to pack it in.

ANDY. What? You can't retire. You're the best teacher they've got. The whole world would fall apart.

JOANNE. Thank you, sweetheart.

ANDY. I mean it. I would be nothing without you. You are the wind beneath my wings.

JOANNE. All right, okay, stop, you're embarrassing me. So, we watched the show last night.

ANDY. Yeah? What'd you think?

JOANNE. It's getting better.

ANDY. You're too kind.

JOANNE. Why do they all wear such expensive sweaters? They're supposed to be middle-class...

ANDY. Is this why you called?

JOANNE. No. Remember the Liebers, from our street?

ANDY. Yeah.

JOANNE. Their son, Daniel, is graduating from Princeton, and he wants to be in show business. He's done a lot of plays.

ANDY. Really.

JOANNE. He's heard all about you. He's moving to L.A.

ANDY. Oh, good, we're running out of ambitious Jewish kids.

JOANNE. Are you being sarcastic?

ANDY. Yes. Does he have any interest in law school?

JOANNE. No, I asked. So, listen, he wants to write to you before he gets there. Can I give him your address?

ANDY. I don't know…

JOANNE. He's a nice kid. Maybe you could help him.

ANDY. Nobody helps anybody. Nobody can. Not the way ya think.

JOANNE. All right, okay. I'll tell his mother you're too busy.

ANDY. No. Wait. Give him my number. I'll take him to lunch.

JOANNE. Thank you. You sure it's not too much trouble?

ANDY. Not at all. I'll tell him what I know.

(The lights fade slowly.)

End of Play.

Also by
Jonathan Tolins...

If Memory Serves

The Twilight of the Golds

Please visit our website **samuelfrench.com** for complete descriptions and licensing information.

www.ingramcontent.com/pod-product-compliance
Lightning Source LLC
Chambersburg PA
CBHW070645300426
44111CB00013B/2277